Modern Monetary Theory and the Recovery

Brian Romanchuk

Published by BondEconomics, Canada

www.BondEconomics.com

© Brian Romanchuk 2021

All rights reserved. No parts of this publication may be reproduced or stored in a retrieval system or transmitted in any form without the prior permission of the author.

Published by BondEconomics, 2021, Montréal Québec.

Nothing in this book constitutes investment or tax advice. Investors are advised to seek professional advice tailored to their situation. Although best efforts have been made to ensure the validity of information contained herein, there is no guarantee of its accuracy or completeness.

Library and Archives Canada

Modern Monetary Theory and the Recovery

Brian Romanchuk 1968-

ISBN 978-1-7751676-9-3 Epub Edition

ISBN 978-1-7751676-8-6 Kindle Edition

ISBN 978-1-7776002-0-4 Paperback Edition

Chapter 1 Contents

Chapter 1	**Overview**..1	
1.1	Introduction	1
1.2	What Is MMT? (Short Version)	1
1.3	MMT Politics	8
1.4	About this Book	11
Chapter 2	**The Era of Sluggish Recoveries**...................................15	
2.1	Introduction	15
2.2	Labour Market Evolution	19
2.3	NAIRU, and Other Will-o'-the-Wisps	26
2.4	The Drift to Austerity	37
2.5	The Rise and Decline of Inflation Targeting	43
Chapter 3	**Doing Better**...49	
3.1	Introduction	49
3.2	Fiscal Policy Reform	49
3.3	The Job Guarantee	53
3.4	Green New Deal	61
3.5	Changing Governmental Financing Procedures	63
3.6	Guessing About the Future	67
Chapter 4	**What Is MMT? (Longer Version)**..............................71	
4.1	Introduction	71
4.2	The Mosler *White Paper*	*72*
4.3	Price Level Determination	75
4.4	Fiscal Sustainability	82
4.5	Theory of Inflation	90
4.6	Broad MMT	96
Chapter 5	**Frequently Raised Critiques**.....................................103	
5.1	Introduction	103
5.2	Non-Answerable Critiques	103

5.3	Rhetorical Tricks (and Money Printing)	105
5.4	Need to Lie to Politicians and Voters	110
5.5	Inflation Worries	114
5.6	Active Fiscal Policy Required?	117
5.7	MMT Ignores the Banking System?	121
5.8	Post-Keynesian Squabbling	126
5.9	Net Financial Asset Skepticism	131
5.10	Only Applicable to United States?	133
5.11	Replication With a Neoclassical Framework?	138
5.12	Nothing New?	141

Index 153

Acknowledgements

I would like to thank the readers of my articles at BondEconomics.com for their feedback. Portions of this text previously appeared as articles on that site, and I have been able to incorporate suggestions and corrections. I would also like to thank Judy Yelon for her editing of this text.

Finally, any errors and omissions are my own.

Chapter 1 Overview

1.1 Introduction

The world stumbled into yet another deep recession in 2020. Although economies are starting to recover from the effects of the pandemic, there are good reasons to fear a repeat of the experience of earlier decades: largely tepid growth in which job creation is weak.

Slow growth in recent decades was not an accident; it was the result of policies that were aimed at suppressing inflation and improving economic efficiency. Although there have been multiple attempts to come up with theories to explain slow growth, the most provocative arguments come from a new school of economic thought – Modern Monetary Theory (MMT).

In this book I discuss the causes of slow growth in the developed world after the early 1990s from a Modern Monetary Theory perspective. Policy proposals from MMT proponents that aim to rejuvenate the labour market without causing a resurgence of inflation will be examined.

Modern Monetary Theory is an outgrowth of the heterodox post-Keynesian school of economics, and the overall scope of the theory is often obscured, or mangled, in popular discussions. This text outlines its key concepts with the objective of reducing confusion.

Given the reality that MMT arguments are hotly debated, this book concludes with a chapter of criticisms of MMT. I am sympathetic to MMT and, therefore, not impartial. However, I believe I provide enough information for the reader to draw their own conclusions, as well as to pursue critiques elsewhere.

I explain MMT concepts in conventional terms, and opinions on topics of interest are offered. As such, this is not a textbook, rather it is a guide that allows the reader to navigate debates as well as glean background information about cited texts. My hope is that if the reader wishes to pursue a particular topic of interest, they are shown where to start digging.

1.2 What Is MMT? (Short Version)

There are two ways of defining MMT: a narrow definition (or *core MMT*), and a broad definition. (This is my preferred wording but probably non-standard, although I have seen references elsewhere to "core MMT.") The two "versions" of MMT are not incompatible, but the "narrow" definition is the minimal version that covers key concepts that set MMT apart from other schools of thought.

Most MMT primers focus on the definition of *narrow MMT*, while many of the interesting questions in economics (which show up in financial macro analysis) end up in *broad MMT*. It should come as no surprise that if you are interested in a topic that falls under the category of broad MMT, watching an online video about narrow MMT will leave a lot of questions unanswered. As such, there is a reasonable scope for good faith misunderstandings of what MMT is about. This section outlines the narrow/broad distinction and offers an initial overview of key points.

Before continuing, I offer this disclaimer. I am presenting this overview from my perspective. The description here is not authoritative, and so it would be a mistake to be concerned with its exact wording. Later chapters give a longer description of MMT and stay closer to source materials. My objective here is to explain concepts in a relatively conventional fashion as a preliminary to later chapters. If the reader reads only this section, they will at least have an inkling of what MMT is about – which is not the case if one reads many descriptions prepared by critics.

Narrow MMT

The narrow version of MMT uses as its base case a fiat currency (and not an alleged barter economy or pegged currency). For a fiat currency, government money is a public monopoly – and analysis and policy should be based on that starting point. The economic reason why governments issue money is to provision themselves easily, instead of demanding goods and services in-kind (e.g., demand that citizens work for the government without pay). *(To be perfectly clear, I am specifying that this is the economic justification for current arrangements; this says nothing about the history of the adoption of money – which I consider part of broad MMT.)*

Fiat currencies mainly exist as electronic entries, and have no inherent value (unlike gold, which has uses in industry and jewelry). To provision itself using money, that money must have value in trading in the non-government sector. The government needs to think like a monopolist and set its policy to ensure that government money has value in exchange.

One leg of the monetary monopolist view of government ends up being similar to what is known as *Functional Finance* (an Old Keynesian school of thought, heavily associated with the economist Abba Lerner.) These

core principles attract a lot of attention in discussions.
- The role of taxes is to create a demand for money to meet tax payment obligations – which are denominated in the domestic currency. There is a real need to pay taxes – since there is a real cost to going to jail for tax avoidance – and so money has a real value. This explains why private actors rationally offer real goods and resources in exchange for electronic entries.
- Since the central government is a monopolist issuer of its money, and that money is not pegged to any external instrument, there is no danger of the central government running out of money. *(This does not apply to sub-sovereigns, nor to central governments that do not control their currency, such as euro area sovereigns.)*
- This means that the central government is not finance constrained like private entities such as households, firms, and sub-sovereigns. (The preferred phrasing is that the central government is the *issuer* of the currency, all those other entities are *users* of the currency.) Government bonds are not economically needed as financing instruments: their economic function is to remove "money" from the banking system (commonly referred to as reserves, although that is a misnomer at this point), to allow for a risk-free yield curve with positive interest rates. (This observation can be very surprising and non-intuitive, but justifying it requires a background discussion of monetary policy operations. This is found in many primers, or my own *Understanding Government Finance*.) The issuance of bonds to drain reserves allows the possibility of using interest rates to influence the economy – a policy lever that MMT proponents feel is much weaker than conventional analysis suggests.
- Instead of a financial constraint, governments face an inflation constraint. That is, the limits of acceptable fiscal policy are determined by the effect on the price level.

The previous leg of argument is well-known and captures most arguments about MMT in popular forums (and even some academic reviews by mainstream economists that cannot be bothered to enquire further into MMT). However, the next leg is more important from the perspective of defining MMT as being distinct from Functional Finance.

The previous discussion assumes that the country is a *currency sovereign*. In the real world, the determination of currency sovereignty is not binary. That is, the control a country has over the currency it borrows in lies on a spectrum. This creates a vagueness when applying the concept to the real world, which creates legitimate debates. I prefer to bypass this vagueness by taking a bond market-centric view: can the country be forced to default by market participants? This risk is complex to analyse, and the determination is a judgement call. The implication is that the definition must be somewhat fuzzy. I discuss default risks in *Understanding Government Finance*.

In addition to using taxes to ensure that the currency has *some* value, governments help determine the value of the currency by the prices they set in their dealings with the private sector. Given that the widespread assumption in economic models is that the government is a price taker, this changes the perspective on some issues.

More specifically, a key observation is that the labour market is the most important domestic market. Conventional economists argue that citizens must be kept unemployed to discipline workers, which is supposed to moderate inflation. However, Bill Mitchell and Warren Mosler independently argued that the government can enact a policy like commodity price support programmes. That is, have a programme that bids for all unused labour at a fixed price. This is known as a Job Guarantee. This conception of the Job Guarantee is a key theoretical development that led MMT to be viewed as a new school of thought.

Other wages in the private sector are then set relative to the Job Guarantee benchmark. Since the post-Keynesian argument is that output prices end up being set as a mark-up over production costs, the Job Guarantee wage ends up being an important component of the determination of the aggregate price level. (Economists had previously discussed similar programmes, but the linkage to price level determination was not emphasised.)

Once these basic principles about fiscal and pricing policy are in place, the focus then switches to *monetary operations* – what exactly is happening in the financial system in the context of government finance? The reality is that each jurisdiction has different legal and regulatory structures, and so a researcher needs to dig into each one independently. The digging keeps coming up with the same answers – although there are self-imposed legal restrictions on government financing, the only true constraint on fiscal policy is inflation, since financial constraints are not truly binding. This is quite different from conventional worries about *financing* government spending.

The discussion of monetary operations runs into the thorny question of "money printing." In just the final weeks of editing this book, I ran into three different assertions by mainstream economists that "MMT was just money printing" (or monetary financing). However, the concept is largely absent from this text (I discuss the debate about the term). This absence suggests that "money printing" is not the core of the theory.

Another part of operations analysis looks at the banking system. The MMT story is straightforward: the conventional banks act as regulated utilities, and so "bank money" is an extension of "government money." This "bank money" is supplemented by other short-term private sector money market instruments that can be treated as "money." The acceptability of these private monies rises and falls with the business cycle; in a crisis, only the core money instruments that are backed by the government are viewed as money.

Another characteristic of MMT writing is an emphasis on sector balances and stock-flow consistent models. Since accounting identities are true by definition, the theoretical value rests more on the interpretation. A key example is that government debt is an asset for other sectors of the economy. Although this should be obvious, this offers a differing perspective on government debt. The prevailing narrative is that government debt is an evil, and so there are no side effects from reducing the amount outstanding. Once we realise that the private sector wants to hold these assets, debt reduction has mixed implications.

From the modelling perspective, the analysis of sectoral balances emphasis is tied to the stock-flow consistent (SFC) modelling approach. Stock-flow consistent models are the preferred idiom for developing post-Keynesian models, and so if one wants to pursue mathematical treatments, that is where one should look.

This largely wraps up what I call narrow MMT. In my opinion, most of these areas of discussion should not be too controversial, but many people are obsessed with how to describe these concepts. For someone new to economics, the previous topics are a lot of ground to cover. My earlier book *Understanding Government Finance* discusses many of these topics in more detail.

However, anyone experienced with macroeconomics would realise that macroeconomics involves more topics than what was listed above. This moves us toward broad MMT.

Broad MMT

When I write "MMT" without qualification, I am almost certainly referring to broad MMT. My guess is that academic MMT proponents agree with this perspective. However, when outsiders discuss "MMT," they only include the academic writings of self-described MMTers and the contents of online primers, and that ends up being closer to what I describe as narrow MMT.

My view of broad MMT is wide – and possibly wider than that of other MMTers. My starting point is to look at what the post-Keynesian academic Marc Lavoie describes as "broad-tent post-Keynesian" thinking. (I use the definition found in Section 1.4.4 of *Post-Keynesian Economics: New Foundations*.) For readers who are unfamiliar with post-Keynesian economics, a key point to keep in mind is that it is a group that split from the mainstream relatively early in the post-World War II era, and was deliberately pushed to the fringes of academia by the 1980s. Correspondingly, post-Keynesians developed a large body of thought in parallel with mainstream neoclassical economics before the advent of MMT proper.

Broad-tent post-Keynesian economics consists of a large number of different groups – not all of whom who agree with each other. (For example, the group that Lavoie defines *as narrow-tent post-Keynesians* argue that the other groups do not qualify as post-Keynesian.) I define *broad MMT* to be the parts of broad-tent post-Keynesian economics that is consistent with the core analysis of *narrow MMT*. This means that it can include research by economists who are critical of MMT elsewhere. Defining the boundaries of what thinking is consistent with core MMT beliefs is going to be a judgement call, and not everyone will agree where the boundaries are (or even whether defining such boundaries is a good idea).

The textbook *Macroeconomics* by William Mitchell, L. Randall Wray, and Martin Watts is the best starting point for understanding broad MMT. However, that text is an undergraduate textbook, and simplifies the academic literature. One needs to dig into monographs and articles for more specialised references. (This text provides a starting point for such references.)

The following is a non-exhaustive list of topics that I have run across

over the years. (This list is biased towards my interests.)
- Labour market analysis and the inflation process. Alternative counter-inflationary policies.
- Business cycle theory.
- Rejection of the assumptions and methodologies of neoclassical economics. (Arguably, too much of post-Keynesian discourse consists of complaining about neoclassical economics.)
- Analysis of fiscal policy.
- History of money (associated with the Chartalist school of thought, many people refer to MMT proponents as "neo-Chartalists").
- Legal and social analysis of the monetary and financial system.
- Analysis of the Job Guarantee, and historical analysis of similar programmes across the globe.
- Analysis of the Green New Deal proposal.
- The challenges faced by developing countries, as well as the difficulties associated with non-floating currencies (especially the euro area).
- Although my interest is exclusively with macroeconomics, the late Fred Lee at the University of Missouri Kansas City was a noted researcher in microeconomics. (UMKC is a stronghold for MMT academics.)

The rest of this text gives a limited introduction to some of these topics. However, it is clear that one would need a graduate level textbook to just introduce these topics. Broad MMT is an entire school of thought of economics, and not just a model like the Quantity *Theory* of Money, or the Fiscal *Theory* of the Price Level. Based on conversations with neoclassical economists, they assume MMT is just a single canonical model like those "theories" that can somehow be slotted into the neoclassical body of thought. In reality, MMT (or the post-Keynesian theoretical project) aims to replace neoclassical theory in its entirety.

Concluding Remarks

Online MMT debates are inherently frustrating. In many cases, critics have a limited grasp on what narrow MMT says, but then they immediately veer into discussing topics that fit within broader MMT. This frustrates good faith discussions. Meanwhile, it is not hard to find bad faith criticisms (e.g., mainstream academics not citing a single academic reference from an MMT source).

References and Further Reading

The remaining sections of this book provide references for introduction to MMT. Only texts referred to explicitly here are now listed.

- *Macroeconomics*, by William Mitchell, L. Randall Wray, and Martin Watts. *Red Globe Press*, 2019. ISBN: 978-1-137-61066-9
- My earlier books *Understanding Government Finance* and *An Introduction to SFC Models Using Python* discuss narrow MMT and stock-flow consistent models, respectively.
- I base my overview of post-Keynesian schools of thought on the discussion found in *Post-Keynesian Economics: New Foundations*, by Marc Lavoie. Edward Elgar Publishing, 2014. ISBN: 978-1-78347-582-7

Note: I would like to thank Twitter user Bob Leore for the suggestion to explicitly include the comments on sectoral balances.

1.3   MMT Politics

When one looks at popular debates, the political economy stance of MMT often comes up. For many partisans of the free market, MMT is often described as "socialist." This largely tells us that many free market partisans are not entirely sure what socialism is, but it is possible to understand where the complaint is coming from.

The first thing to note is that Modern Monetary Theory – as a theory – matches what is called "bipartisan" in the United States. The idea is that the *theory* is politically neutral with respect to mainstream politics. (I explain the distinction between "bipartisan" and "neutral" below.) Nevertheless, I think it is a very safe bet that most visible MMT activists and academics would be considered progressive.

This is not an accident. Fiscal conservatives – as the name suggests – are typically associated with conservative (or free market) parties. Modern Monetary Theory largely contradicts the beliefs of fiscal conservatism. As such, the theory is going to be more attractive to progressives, and there was a natural snowballing effect. (With an MMT conference full of progressives, free marketeers might skip the next one.)

However, if we look at actual policies, it is not hard to find free market parties that only pay lip service to fiscal conservatism. (Such as the Republican party in the United States, and the Mulroney era Progressive Conservatives in Canada.) These parties are happy to increase defence appropriations and cut taxes, without any concerns about the sacredness of the debt-to-GDP ratio. The evils of government indebtedness are only re-discovered when the other party is in power, or when it is necessary to find reasons to cut programme spending. As such, it would be surprising to see free market parties rushing out to endorse MMT, but at the same time, those parties are not exactly projecting a coherent vision for fiscal policy. From the perspective of a rates market participant, holding an incoherent view that can generate losing trades – the famous example being the Widowmaker Trade in Japanese Government Bonds – is not attractive.

Policies: Not Libertarian, But…

Like most MMT proponents, I argue that MMT as a theory offers a somewhat neutral way of viewing the world, and by itself does not demand that certain policies be implemented. However, the theory does indicate that certain policy options are better than others, and unsurprisingly, most MMT proponents support them. These policies are generally not going to be attractive to libertarians (particularly fans of Austrian economics), but non-libertarian pro-market politicians used to exist. I will highlight some of the policies that are of interest, without delving into what they are (as they are discussed later in the book).

- The starting point for MMT is that it highlights the policy space enjoyed by floating currency sovereigns. As such, the theory is slanted towards a preference to floating currency values. One may note that not having price controls is normally viewed as the free market position, but we have the historical accident that libertarians demand that the government peg the value of gold. From the other side, many leftists assume that the preference for a floating currency value implies *laissez-faire* policies toward trade and capital controls, but this is not the case – you can have capital controls, and still let the currency value float. That said, MMT proponents are generally not worried about U.S. trade deficits, a position often seen as being pro-free trade. (By contrast, a significant number of commentators were worried about the "financing" of the U.S. current account deficit before 2008, and they expected that to trigger a crisis.)

- The Job Guarantee (described in Section 3.3) is a proposed social programme that unsurprisingly guarantees everyone a job at a fixed wage. (Although similar policies have existed, no universal programme that matches the desired design has been implemented.) This is obviously not going to make libertarians happy, but at the same time, it would effectively replace other social welfare programmes. Old school conservatives were always unhappy paying people to do nothing.
- The other well-known policy is the Green New Deal (Section 3.4), which is popular among MMT proponents, and would normally be viewed as "progressive." However, this is a key case where we need to distinguish between the theory of MMT, and the views of proponents. The core of MMT is economics, and not environmental science, and so the scientific justification for the Green New Deal is outside the theory. Instead, the role of MMT is to describe how to marshal the resources for the programme. Since other economic theories could be assigned the same task, this is not exclusively associated to MMT.
- MMT suggests that things like fiscal rules and worries about the debt-to-GDP ratio are nonsensical. As such, it is not really an MMT policy, rather an anti-policy (the policy is to ignore people who propose fiscal rules). MMT recognises that inflation is a constraint on fiscal policy, and that observation should not be inherently political. In practice it is, since free market parties have hitched their wagon to naïve fiscal conservatism.
- Within MMT, there is a preference for fiscal policy to monetary policy. This is only a political stance because the neoliberal consensus went the other way, although one could try to tie this to the size of the governmental sector. (A government that is normally only 5% of GDP will have a hard time stabilising aggregate demand with fiscal policy.)

Bipartisan Versus Neutral

The reason why I describe the theory as "bipartisan" and not "neutral" is because it does incorporate the *status quo* with respect to capitalism. Since the theory involves money and a split between a private sector and a public sector, private property has not been abolished.

The result is that despite the complaints from fans of the free market that "MMT is socialist," we also see MMT being assailed from the left. My personal favourites are the complaints from "sound finance socialists," as being a "sound finance socialist" seems inherently silly. I have seen arguments that MMT is being financed by hedge fund billionaire(s) as a means to push for lower tax rates.

Politics Are Not My Concern
I am not blind to the political considerations of what I am writing about, and I do not pretend to be neutral. However, I do not want other people telling me how to vote, and I extend the same courtesy. My politics are somewhat archaic – old-school Canadian Prairie Populist – and I am living in the most developed social welfare state in North America. In Québec, we have all the things that American progressives are demanding, including socialised health care, low cost higher education, legalised cannabis, and high marginal tax rates. As such, I can afford to take a somewhat detached attitude towards these affairs.

From a theoretical perspective, my bias is to present MMT as politically neutral. I would like MMT to shift towards the dominant paradigm within academic economics, but it seems straightforward that this will not happen if it is seen as tied to one end of the political spectrum. This is not just the inherent conservatism of economic institutions – which they are – but the reality that the mainstream political parties need to have a common language to debate policy options. At present, neoclassical economics provides that common language, and I view this as the reason why it has not been dislodged.

1.4 About this Book

Most of this book was published earlier as articles on the website BondEconomics.com. This was done to get feedback from readers before publication.

The target reading difficulty is set at an intermediate level, with the intention of being relatively close to what one might see in the business press or financial markets research. It is certainly more advanced than many of the other MMT popular primers. I am assuming that the reader is familiar with economic jargon and has a rough idea of recent financial and economic history. My target audience is readers with some knowledge of economics, but unfamiliar with MMT literature.

To avoid some formatting issues that have come from publication across three editions (two electronic formats, plus paperback), I have eliminated equations, and dropped the use of footnotes and endnotes. (The loss of the ability to make snarky comments in footnotes was unfortunate.) Instead, I have placed select references at the end of each section. This is probably the most useful for non-academic readers, but it does imply that certain books or articles will have their bibliographic information repeated several times within the text. Since I am not charging by the word, this repetition does not really matter.

I am writing as a populariser, but I am not afraid of expressing my opinions. Readers should not view everything I write as reflecting a hypothetical MMT party line. I generally try to make clear what are my opinions versus what I see as the consensus. Obviously, if one wants to discern the MMT party line, the quotes I provide, as well as the various references, are the sources to turn to.

There is a chapter of MMT criticism in which I have tried to describe the complaints using my usual terminology, while not following the theoretical biases of the critics. I do not want to get bogged down with explaining non-MMT economics. I tried to give a good faith overview of the complaints, but there is no doubt that I disagree with most of the complaints.

One of the theoretical tics of MMT academics is their concern about the verbal framing of concepts. They are reasonably unhappy with how mainstream economists have smuggled political baggage into what is supposed to be "neutral" and "scientific" discourse. Although I see those concerns about framing as being valid, my main concern is making myself understood, and so I may use framing that they might not be happy with.

Labelling Issues

One of the issues of describing the debates around MMT is the issue of distinguishing it from other schools of thought. The problem is the dominant school of thought, which is typically labelled "mainstream." Since "mainstream" is a description of how widespread a view is, it is ambiguous, and I generally try to avoid using it. I use *neoclassical* to refer to the dominant math-heavy version of economic theory that currently dominates elite universities, which is typically based around dynamic stochastic general equilibrium (DSGE) models. This might be a stretch of the term "neoclassical" versus its technical meaning, but that seems to be the best and most widely understood label.

I distinguish *conventional* economics from this neoclassical theory, although there is a vague relationship between the two. Conventional economics is short for the conventional wisdom (a phrase coined by John Kenneth Galbraith in *The Affluent Society*, although the sources of conventional wisdom have shifted). Conventional thinking about economics is largely based on ideas that feature prominently in Economics 101 textbooks, and are often spouted by bank economists, rating agency employees, politicians, and other financial commentators. One might call this "Economics 101ism."

Neoclassical academics can be quite irate when their thinking is lumped in with musings from financial market commentators. To be fair, few academics want to be associated with some of the logic that is put forth in financial market commentary, regardless of the school of thought. Nevertheless, very few people outside of academia voluntarily read academic journals, and "Economics 101ism" is the school of thought that is visible in public debates. The fact that conventional economics is heavily based on undergraduate textbooks written by neoclassical academics, and that the reality that opinion pieces from senior academics are often indistinguishable from Economics 101ism makes it difficult to draw a firm line between these groups. My argument is that the neoclassicals are happy to accept the prestige of teaching at elite universities, but are unwilling to take ownership of the fact that their students consistently spout nonsense in public.

One final point is the question of what to call supporters of MMT. One quite often sees "MMTers" (although "MMTist" – short for "modern monetary theorist" is perhaps better). Since "MMTers" is inelegant in text, I went with the stilted "MMT proponent." I switch between "modern monetary theory" and "MMT" based on what looks better.

Publication Timing

This text was largely written in early-to-mid 2020, during the initial pandemic lockdown. Figures reflect data that had just been disrupted. The final edits were started in November 2020, just after the U.S. presidential election (and with election results still being disputed in the courts). Since I am not making specific forecasts, I have not attempted to make last-minute adjustments based on political or economic developments. .

A second wave of COVID-19 infections is now hitting many developed economies (although certain economies have managed to effectively eradicate the disease). Given the uncertainty about the effects of this wave, I did not see updating the data by a few months as being useful. The risk of updating the figures is that the text might contradict what is being shown, which could ultimately be more confusing to readers than the missing data. This is a book, and any comments I make about "current" conditions will be rapidly out of date. My objective in my final editing pass is to eliminate unclear text, and making last minute content changes is not compatible with this.

It is possible that the outcome of the American elections will change the political outlook that I have outlined here, but my political forecasts might prove more embarrassing than leaving my text somewhat out of date.

Chapter 2 The Era of Sluggish Recoveries

2.1 Introduction

If we look at the post-1990 era in the developed world, we see a relatively similar pattern: long expansions with relatively low economic volatility, punctuated with short recessions. In fact, in the case of Australia, the expansion was only put to an end by the Pandemic of 2020. However, if we look past the low volatility, we also see that growth rates were relatively low, and employment conditions generally weak.

The uniformity of experiences was greater in the "Anglo" countries; Japan and euro area countries had somewhat divergent conditions. Japan had an investment boom run out of stem in the mid-1990s, while the euro area countries had a "euro convergence boom" that was the side effect of lower interest rates in countries that previously had weak currencies. That said, conditions converged after the 2001 global technology recession.

This moderation of economic volatility was famously labelled "The Great Moderation" by Ben Bernanke in a speech in 2004. Bernanke was at the time a governor of the Federal Reserve and later became the chair of the Federal Open Market Committee. The concept of The Great Moderation was mocked after The Financial Crisis (e.g., see the article by Bill Mitchell in the references section), but I would argue that we can at least characterise this era as having a commonality of long-lived, sluggish recoveries.

Sluggishness Not Expected
One of the interesting aspects of these sluggish recoveries was that they were not expected by the consensus. The conventional view ascribes great importance to central bank policy, and low policy rates were expected to generate a rapid recovery from recessions.

U.S. 5-Year Treasury Versus Realised Short Rate

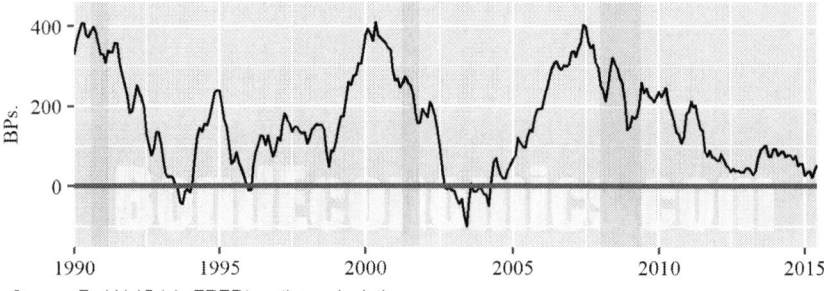

Source: Fed H.15 (via FRED), author calculations.

Giving an objective measure of the consensus view is somewhat awkward. I will focus on bond yields, as they are inherently forward-looking. The explanation for this forward-looking behaviour is that bond investors expect that a bond should provide at least as high a return as holding money-market instruments. The figure above illustrates the historical experience in the United States (the experience in other developed markets tended to be similar).

The top panel shows the 5-year Treasury yield, which is compared to the average of the Fed Funds target rate over the subsequent five years (labelled "realised short rate"). Since the realised rate at a given date requires knowing the level of Fed Funds over the next five years, the time series ends in 2015. The bottom panel shows the spread between those rates, in basis points (1 basis point = 0.01%). What the figure shows is that the 5-year yield over the 1990 to 2015 period was generally greater than the realised short rate. (The implication is that bonds outperformed cash, so this was a secular bond bull market.)

We can focus on the periods at the end of shaded recession bars. At those time points, we saw small rises in yields (bond bear markets), and an extremely large positive spread between the 5-year yield and the realised path of short rates over the next five years. The explanation was straightforward: bond market participants believed that rate cuts were excessive, and that the economy would recover quickly. This did not happen, and bond yields drifted lower. The only times that the 5-year Treasury yield fell below realised short-term rates was once the economy stagnated, and bond market participants got too exuberant in extrapolating low policy rates.

I started working in finance in 1998, and I can attest that being bearish on bonds was the default view for strategists from 1998 to 2012 (or so). *(There were cyclical swings towards bullishness, typically after bond yields already fell.)* The default bearishness by strategists started to fade by 2012, once the magnitude of the collapse in activity created by the Financial Crisis of 2008 sunk in (and the economic drag created by the crisis in the euro periphery). It was only then that the consensus accepted that the U.S. economy could be stuck in a slow growth path, even with interest rates below the rate of inflation ("negative real rates") and so-called "money-printing" by the Federal Reserve. One important thing to note is that MMT started to gain prominence at about that time, and part of the attractiveness of the theory was that it offered a more coherent explanation why monetary policy fizzled.

Why Bond Yields Instead of Surveys?

One might question the use of bond yields as a measure of consensus — why not a survey of economists?

My initial concern is the difficulty of displaying the data in a useful format. It is easy to show a time history of GDP growth up to a certain date, and then forecasts of its path. Unfortunately, that just shows expectations at one point in time. What I want to highlight is the pervasive over-optimism that infected the forecasting community, and so we would need look at multiple forecasts, and the resulting graph is hard for newcomers to interpret. By contrast, the bond yield/realised yield spread offers a summary of forecast errors as a single time series.

The next issue is a concern with the quality of consensus economist forecasts. Economists in the surveys play games, and herd together in a dysfunctional fashion. They face limited criticism if their forecast is incorrect. Conversely, bond investors have "skin in the game," as their bonus (or even job) is at risk if they mis-price securities.

Term Premium

The term premium is a subject that often comes up in the concept of discussing rate expectations. Technically, we should expect the 5-year yield to be higher than the realised average of short-term rates by the term premium (which varies over time). However, I do not find an estimate of a term premium of over 200 basis points to be plausible for a 5-year Treasury note, while that is the level of outperformance that we see at the end of recession periods. The reality is that market participants as well as the economist consensus expected rapid turnarounds that were not realised, and the raw outperformance of 5-year bonds gives us a good feel for the magnitude of the forecast miss, even if the term premium slightly adjusts the numbers.

Concluding Remarks

At the time of finishing this book, it is hard to characterise the consensus view. It appears fair to say that commentators are less inclined to believe rapid renormalisation stories than in previous cycles. Conversely, it is not controversial to argue that there could be a rapid mechanical bounce in activity in 2021 as vaccination coverage spreads. Finally, there are signals from the incoming Biden administration that there will be a more comprehensive economic relief package passed. I certainly did not expect such outcome when writing this book, and so my tone herein may have turned out to be too pessimistic.

The next sections will turn to the economic characteristics of modern expansions.

References and Further Reading
- The "Great Moderation" speech by Ben S. Bernanke, made on February 20, 2004. URL:https://www.federalreserve.gov/boarddocs/speeches/2004/20040220/. Bill Mitchell wrote a critique of The Great Moderation in a blog: http://bilbo.economicoutlook.net/blog/?p=7554
- I discuss the relationship between bond yields and expectations in *Understanding Government Finance* and *Interest Rate Cycles: An Introduction*.

2.2 Labour Market Evolution

My argument is that changes in structure in the labour markets that started in the 1980s – but kicked into gear in the early 1990s – explain the structural breaks in the behaviour of the developed economies that took place in the early 1990s. The advantage of these changes has been the decline in inflation. Although neoclassical economists attribute this change to the switch to inflation targeting (as will be discussed in Section 2.5), I do not think we can assume away the changes to the labour markets. The disadvantage of these changes has been the persistent sluggishness in developed economies.

This section is inspired by the book *Full Employment Abandoned: Shifting Sands and Policy Failures*, by Bill Mitchell and Joan Muysken. That text is an advanced academic text, and examines the history of employment policy from an MMT perspective. This section cannot hope to cover the historical analysis of labour markets in Parts I and II of that book. The third part of the book discusses topics that are more widely associated with MMT, and which I will cover elsewhere in this text. If a reader wants a formalised academic textbook that is an introduction to MMT, *Full Employment Abandoned* is one possibility.

The Full Employment Framework

From a long-term perspective, there are two structural changes to the labour market of interest. The first is the movement towards a *full employment framework* in the aftermath of World War II. *Full Employment Abandoned* points to the 1948 Universal Declaration of Human Rights, where Article 23 included the text "Everyone has the right to work, to free choice of employment, to just and favourable conditions of work, and to protection against unemployment."

The next structural change effectively represents an effort to undo the previous changes. Mitchell and Muysken argue that the *OECD Jobs Study: Facts, Analysis, Strategies* of 1994 captured the new consensus perfectly (and provided the role model for reforms). They offer this quotation as a key summary of the thinking:

> [I]t is an inability of OECD economies to adapt rapidly and innovatively to a world of rapid structural change that is the principal cause of high and persistent unemployment... Consequently, the main thrust of the study was directed towards identifying the institutions, rules and regula-

tions, and practices which have weakened the capacity of OECD countries to adapt and innovate, and to search for appropriate policy responses...

To many readers steeped in the current labour policy consensus, the statements by the authors of the OECD report might seem unremarkable. However, they bury key differences from the earlier framework. The core difference is that they view persistent unemployment as being a matching problem (i.e., match the worker and the employer), and not the result of inadequate demand. This difference in the diagnosis implies a different remedy: remove frictions that slow down matching. As was typical for the neoliberal era, regulations were viewed as a source of problems. Meanwhile, one hidden implication is that unemployment is largely the fault of workers – they are not adaptable (e.g., skilled).

Changing Behaviour of the Labour Market

I would say that it is safe to say that there have been considerable qualitative changes in the developed economy labour markets since the 1980s, with the aggregate changes slanted in favour of employers versus workers. Opportunities for women and minorities appear to have improved over that period (which is likely country-specific, so harder to generalise about), so not all the qualitative changes were negative for workers. The problem with discussing qualitative changes is that they are not easily summarised, and the summaries can be the result of political disputes.

The text *Full Employment Abandoned* is focused on the changes in the labour market, and therefore has the space to cover the qualitative changes to the labour market. In this context, Section 5.2 – "The Full Employability Framework" – discusses the changes to labour market programmes that corresponded to the *OECD Jobs Study* world view. The authors state: "The full employability framework allegedly prepares the unemployed worker for paid employment as opposed to providing the policy environment that ensures there are enough jobs." Market-based outcomes are the key to the full employability framework. For example, regional unemployment is to be dealt with via migratory responses by workers (the "get on your bike" philosophy associated with British Conservative politician Norman Tebbit). As Mitchell and Muysken note, relying on migration benefits growing regions, and does little for the development of regions with weak economies.

The Era of Sluggish Recoveries

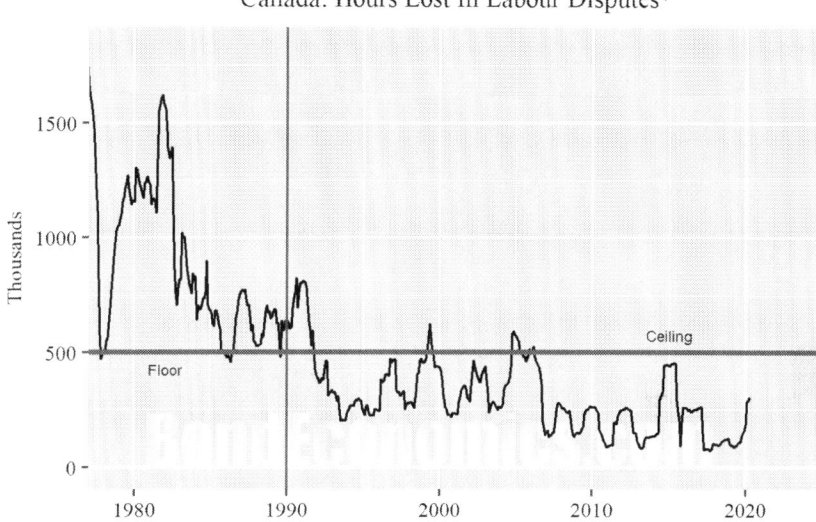

Canada: Hours Lost In Labour Disputes*

*12-month moving average. Source: Statscan.

Since qualitative changes are hard to summarise, we will focus on some quantitative measures of labour market changes. The first example of a quantitative metric is the number of strikes. The figure above shows the hours lost in labour disputes in Canada in a month, smoothed by taking the average over 12 months. Note that I have made no attempt to adjust for the size of the labour force – that grew over the period. We can see the high levels of strikes at the tail end of the 1970s and early 1980s, which were memorable. (One of the annual rituals was trying to mail Christmas cards before a potential postal carrier strike.) I added two somewhat arbitrary lines to illustrate the change in trends. Before 1990, the (smoothed) strike series rarely dipped below 500,000 hours per month. Once we are past the early 1990s, the 500,000-hour line was the effective peak of the smoothed series. (I put the vertical line at 1990 for ease of comparison across figures.) As the chart text observes, the floor for strike activity levels before 1990 became the ceiling thereafter.

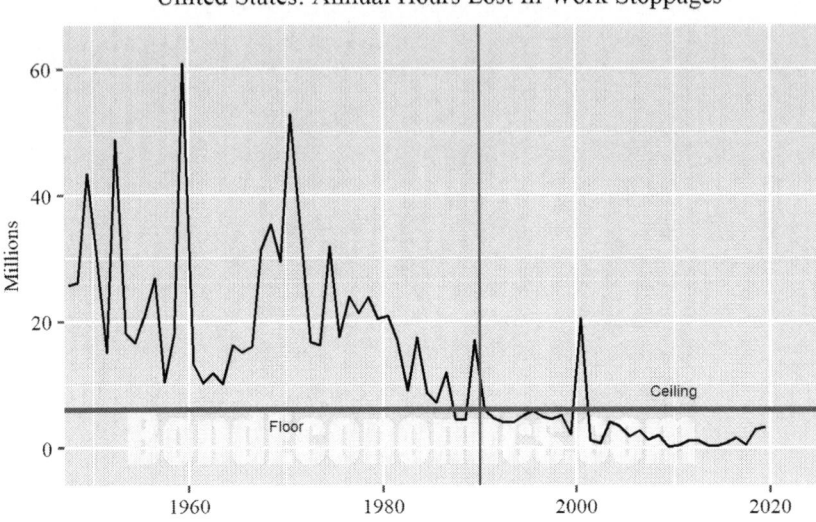

The drop in strike activity was not confined to Canada. As the figure above demonstrates, work stoppages remained relatively low after 1990 (with a single spike in the year 2000). The American data has a longer run of history than the Canadian data, and we can see that rise in strike activity in the late 1960s and 1970s – the era of high inflation.

A closely related trend is the decline in unionisation. Before the 1990s, industries were dominated by large firms with large, unionised workforces. However, starting in the 1980s, firms started shrinking their workforces, outsourcing functions to specialised firms. That outsourcing increasingly moved to countries with lower wages in response to free trade agreements. Currently, the largest unions tend to be associated with government employment, while many large employers (e.g., retailers, fast food) have managed to avoid the unionisation of their workforces.

Long-Term Unemployment

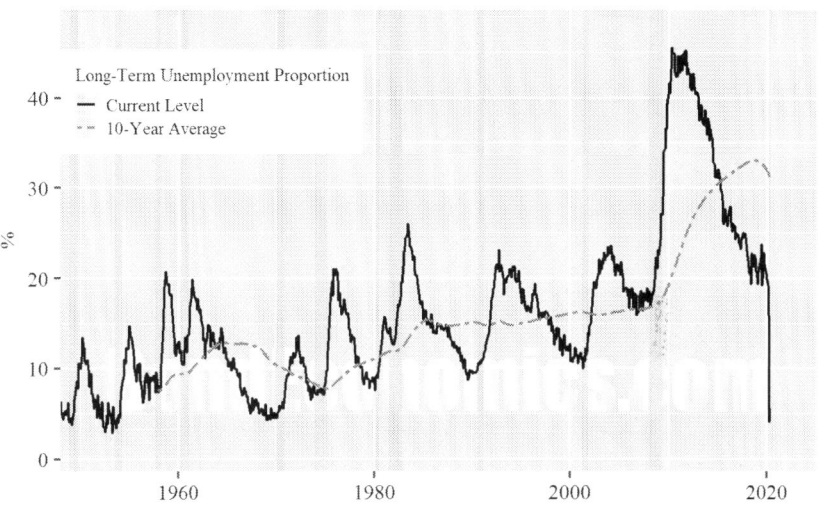

U.S.: Percentage Of Unemployed That Are Long-Term Unemployed*

*Greater than 27 weeks. Shade indicats NBER recessions. Source: BLS (via FRED).

The nature of unemployment has also changed over time, which can be readily seen in the data. The chart above shows how unemployment has become more persistent in the United States. It shows the percentage of the unemployed population that has been unemployed for more than 27 weeks. We see that this percentage rises as the economy comes out of recession, and the most sought-after employees find jobs in the immediate bounce in hiring. The percentage then grinds lower during the expansion, as either long-term unemployed either find a job due to improving conditions, or they drop out of the labour force.

If we look at the 10-year average of the series (which smooths out the effect of recessions), we see an upward slope starting in the 1970s, but without a noticeable deterioration starting in 1990. That said, the measure rose rapidly after the Financial Crisis, and only ground down to 20% during the expansion – which was the peak level in earlier eras.

(The rapidity of the collapse of employment in 2020 meant that most unemployed workers were newly unemployed, and so this ratio returned to levels last seen in the 1970s. My assumption is that this ratio will head higher in response to the initial return to work in the United States.)

Pavlina R. Tcherneva highlighted this ratio in "Reorienting Fiscal Policy: A Critical Assessment of Fiscal Fine-Tuning," which was published in 2013. It offers another analysis of the changing nature of fiscal and job creation policies from an MMT perspective.

Under-Employment

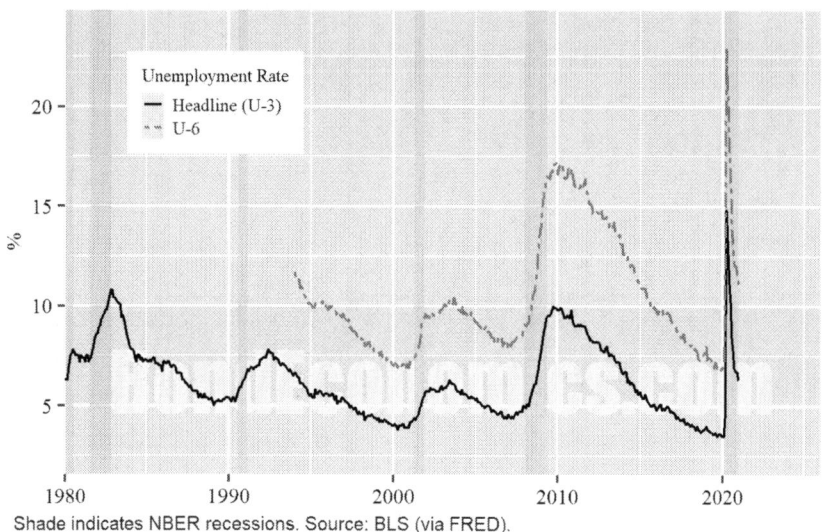

U.S.: Unemployment And Underemployment Rates
Shade indicates NBER recessions. Source: BLS (via FRED).

One final concern with labour market structure is persistent under-employment. These are workers that are considered employed (and are therefore not part of the headline unemployment rate), but they are not working as many hours as they would wish (e.g., working part-time, but wish to have full-time employment). In the United States, there are a number of unemployment definitions, with U-3 being the headline rate (the number that is quoted in headlines), and U-6 being a wide measure of under-employment. These are shown in the figure above. Unfortunately, the U-6 under-employment measure only starts in the mid-1990s, and so we cannot infer anything about structural changes relative to earlier eras.

The rise of the so-called "gig economy" has taken the concept of "adaptability" to the limit. Workers are re-branded "contractors," and would be considered employed (self-employed), even if they work very few hours. Admittedly, there are many cases where people want to be self-employed on a part-time basis – I am in that category – but the status of being "employed" is losing its significance.

Consequences

The reduction in the bargaining power of workers had the effect of lowering inflation rates, consistent with post-Keynesian economic theory. Also, post-Keynesian theory suggests that there would be a reduction in aggregate demand, lowering growth rates. This is consistent with the observed slowness of recovery. Note that this is different than standard neoclassical models that suggest that growth rates ought to bounce around some equilibrium level, and that by reducing frictions in the labour market, growth should have been faster.

Another popular line of argument is that slow wage growth has been associated with greater inequality, and more unequal societies grow more slowly. The mechanism appears straightforward: the ultra-rich spend less of their income, and so hoarding of income increases. The lower propensity to consume lowers aggregate demand. Although this line of argument appears plausible, I am not highlighting it here, as it is not particularly associated with MMT, and faces some empirical issues that would be a distraction.

The next section will return to the relationship between the labour market and inflation. In particular, how the relationship between NAIRU and inflation broke down. The difficulties faced by mainstream economists in this respect represent a large part of the contents of *Full Employment Abandoned*, and we will return to discussing that text.

References and Further Reading

- *Full Employment Abandoned: Shifting Sands and Policy Failures*, William Mitchell and Joan Muysken, Edward Elgar Publishing, 2008. ISBN: 978-1-85898-507-7
- *The OECD Jobs Study: Facts, Analysis, Strategies,* Organisation for Economic Cooperation and Development, 1994.
- "Reorienting Fiscal Policy: A Critical Assessment of Fiscal Fine-Tuning," by Pavlina R. Tcherneva, Levy Economics Institute Working Paper Number 772, 2013. URL: http://www.levyinstitute.org/pubs/wp_772.pdf

2.3 NAIRU, and Other Will-o'-the-Wisps

The discussion of unemployment is a key theoretical divide between Modern Monetary Theory and mainstream approaches. Theoretical conclusions determine the suggested policy response of governments to unemployment. The structural changes to the labour market made by policymakers in the 1990s were the result of following a theory.

The modern version of the theory relied upon the concept of the Non-Accelerating Inflation Rate of Unemployment – NAIRU – although if one digs into academic history, there are a few related measures with slightly different definitions. Since I want to focus on MMT – and avoid being distracted by critiques of neoclassical macro – I want to underline this section is offering a simplified version of the evolution of the concept. Interested readers are pointed to the text *Full Employment Abandoned: Shifting Sands and Policy Failures* by William Mitchell and Joan Muysken. From my perspective, the historical development of these concepts might be of interest to historians of economic thought, but from an empirical perspective, any measure like NAIRU is found to be of little use in understanding the economy. Within the physical sciences and engineering, teachers avoid confusing students by spending excessive amounts of time on defunct theories.

Really Short History of NAIRU

The history behind NAIRU is long, and to do it properly one would need to watch the full evolution of economic theory. Rather than attempt to do that, I am going to focus on the political economy aspects. I will caution the reader that it is simplistic, but my argument is that you need to grasp the big picture before being bogged down in who said what.

I will offer an over-simplified version of pre-Keynesian – often labelled "classical" – thinking. This summary is undoubtedly a caricature of those earlier thinkers' views, but I believe that it captures the spirit of the situation. (*Full Employment Abandoned* delves into this history, and the theory is more nuanced than suggested here. I have little expertise in pre-Keynesian economics, and this short summary captures the spirit of how many Keynesians view the history.) The working assumption was that all markets moved to equilibrium courtesy of the laws of supply and demand. The implication was that unemployment was essentially a natural outcome of market processes, and there was little to be done about it. If the economy is perturbed by some disturbance (a depression or recession), it will move on its own back to the level where all workers who want to work at the prevailing wage are employed. (Since the theory referred to equilibrium, and macroeconomic data were not collected, time scales for adjustments were vague. We still see such vagueness in discussions when economists invoke the "short run" or the "long run.")

The simplified story then continues to suggest that John Maynard Keynes largely created macroeconomics as a separate area of enquiry within economics when he launched his theoretical research programme into the business cycle. (Once again, this summary is oversimplified, and other economists developed macro theory in parallel.) A key insight of this new research programme was that unemployment rates can stagnate at a level above what would be viewed as an "economically efficient" equilibrium. As a result, governments had an imperative to drive down the unemployment rate to the efficient level. This is the Full Employment framework described in Section 2.2.

Free market-oriented politicians and economists were not happy with the social programmes aimed to reduce unemployment, and eventually launched a counterattack. The main theoretical concept advanced was the natural rate of unemployment, proposed by Milton Friedman. The idea is straightforward: if the unemployment rate falls below the natural rate, the economy will experience accelerating inflation. Although Friedman cautioned that the word "natural" was derived from usage elsewhere in economics, it was effectively misinterpreted as being a "law of nature" and immutable. (Friedman did argue that the rate depended on other factors.)

(From the perspective of MMT, this episode is a useful example of the concept of the framing of terminology in economics. Why call it the "natural rate" if it is not really a law of nature? One could easily assume that this was an attempt to mislead the broad public.)

The original formulation of the natural rate of unemployment failed miserably as an empirical concept. Nevertheless, new variants of the concept appeared. In North America, the concept of NAIRU was the most popular replacement. (European theory diverged slightly, following the path set in the text *Unemployment: Macroeconomic Performance and the Labour Market*, by Layard, Nickell, and Jackman. I will stick to the consensus North American version of the theory for simplicity.)

NAIRU: the U.S. Experience

If one looks at the historical debates about NAIRU (and its relations), it is easy to drown in detail. However, if we focus on the post-1990 period, it becomes much easier to discuss. The issue is straightforward: the concept failed empirically. This was not the case in earlier decades: failed models were replaced by models that offered at least temporary improvements.

For reasons of simplicity, I will look at a single measure of NAIRU: the long-term NAIRU produced by the Congressional Budget Office (CBO). It is extremely likely that one could find a different measure that performs slightly better, but that is clearing an extremely low bar.

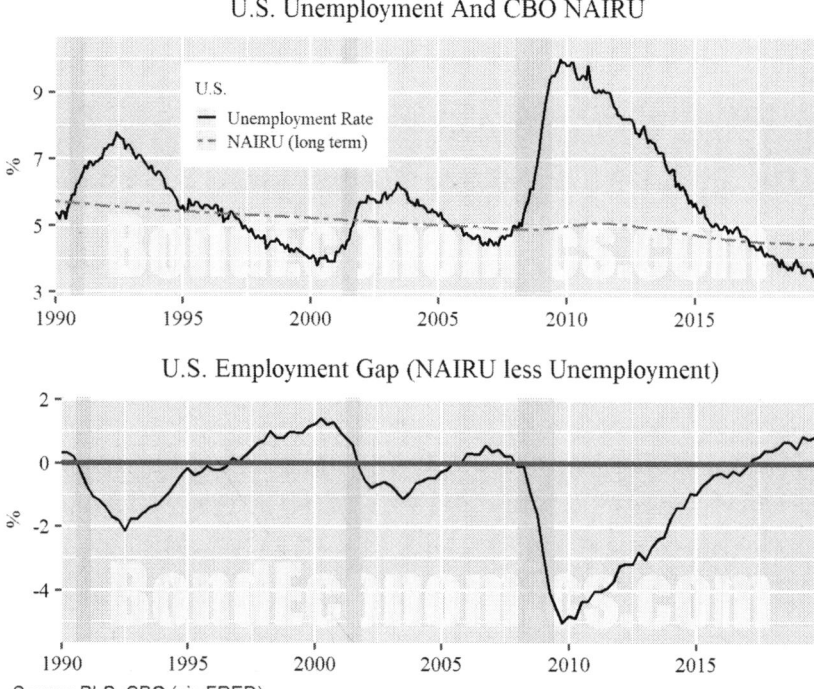

Source: BLS, CBO (via FRED).

The figure above shows the movements of NAIRU and the U-3 (headline) unemployment rate. The top panel shows the levels since 1990, while the bottom shows the difference – NAIRU minus the unemployment rate. (It seems preferable to subtract NAIRU from the unemployment rate, but I am reversing it for reasons to be discussed below.) I am labelling this difference the "employment gap" – as an analogy to the output gap – but I warn that this may not be standard terminology. I cut off the charts in January 2020 to avoid the jump in 2020, which obscures movements in earlier decades.

As can be seen, the unemployment rate spikes higher during recessions, and then grinds steadily lower during the following expansion. (The 2020 experience is likely to be erratic due to the nature of the slowdown. At the time of writing, only a few post-pandemic data points are available.) The unemployment rate slices through the relatively slow-moving NAIRU.

Keep in mind that there are many ways in which one could calculate a NAIRU estimate. However, the premise is that it is a slow-moving variable, similar to the CBO measure shown. If we replaced the CBO NAIRU estimate with any variable that meets that criterion, all that would happen is that the unemployment gap measure just shifts up or down by a certain amount, but the qualitative picture would be the same. That is, the unemployment rate drives below the new series during the expansion, and then shoots above it during the recession. (If the measure was always above or always below the observed unemployment rate, something is obviously wrong.)

Just a simple visual analysis of this chart largely puts to rest an ancient theoretical debate: does the unemployment rate "naturally" converge to NAIRU? Given that it typically took around half a decade to close the negative employment gap after recessions, the reversion speed is too slow to be of any interest.

NAIRU and Inflation

Modern theories of the NAIRU (and its relations) suggest that the employment gap ought to be a determining factor for inflation. The initial problem is that "inflation" is somewhat vague: in this context, one could either look at wage inflation, or the rise of consumer prices (e.g., the CPI). (Yet another alternative is the GDP deflator, but the GDP deflator has some unusual properties that I do not want to deal with.)

If one delves into the economic literature (including *Full Employment Abandoned*), whether one uses consumer price inflation or wage inflation matters if one looks at the historical development of models (who gets credit for what). Since these models have obvious weaknesses, I am not too concerned about these distinctions. For completeness, I will show both variants.

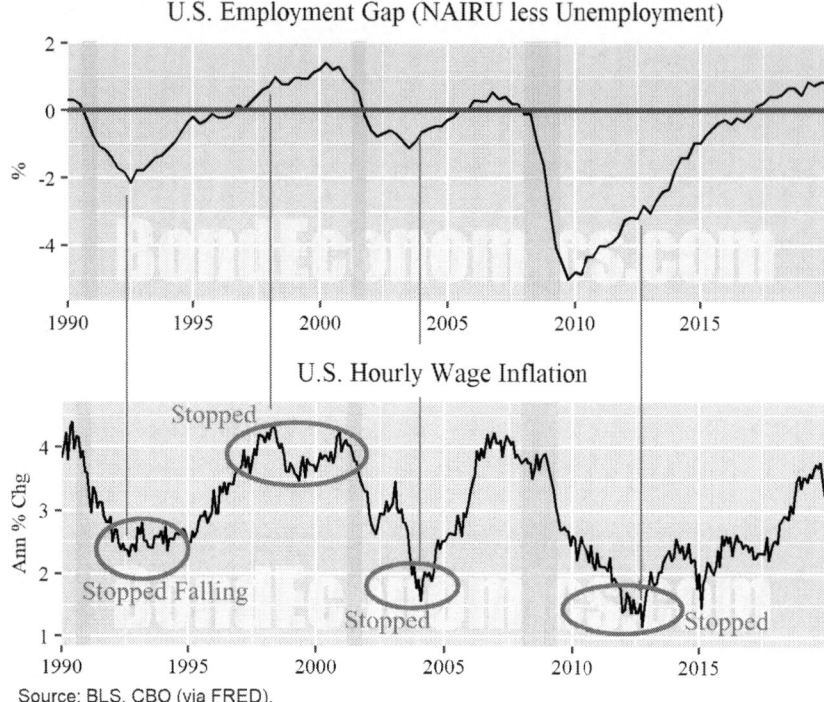

Source: BLS, CBO (via FRED).

The chart above shows the experience of the employment gap and the changes in average hourly earnings in the United States since 1990. The top panel shows the employment gap (NAIRU minus the unemployment rate), and the bottom panel shows the annual change in average hourly earnings.

One initial reaction is that the two series are correlated (the two series move up and down together). This is exactly what one would expect if wage inflation is correlated with the business cycle – which is a prediction of most plausible economic models.

However, this is not enough – we need to see whether inflation is accelerating (since accelerating is the "A" in NAIRU). As we can see, this is not happening. Wage inflation bottoms after a recession, but it does not keep falling. If we look at the three circled episodes after recessions, wage inflation stopped falling when the employment gap was negative – which means that it did not keep falling, even though the employment gap was still negative for a few years. As for a positive acceleration, the one clean episode where the employment gap was clearly positive (in the 1990s), we see that wage inflation stopped accelerating years before the recession (and the employment gap was positive). (The employment gap did not get very positive in the latter two expansions, so the picture is not particularly clear.)

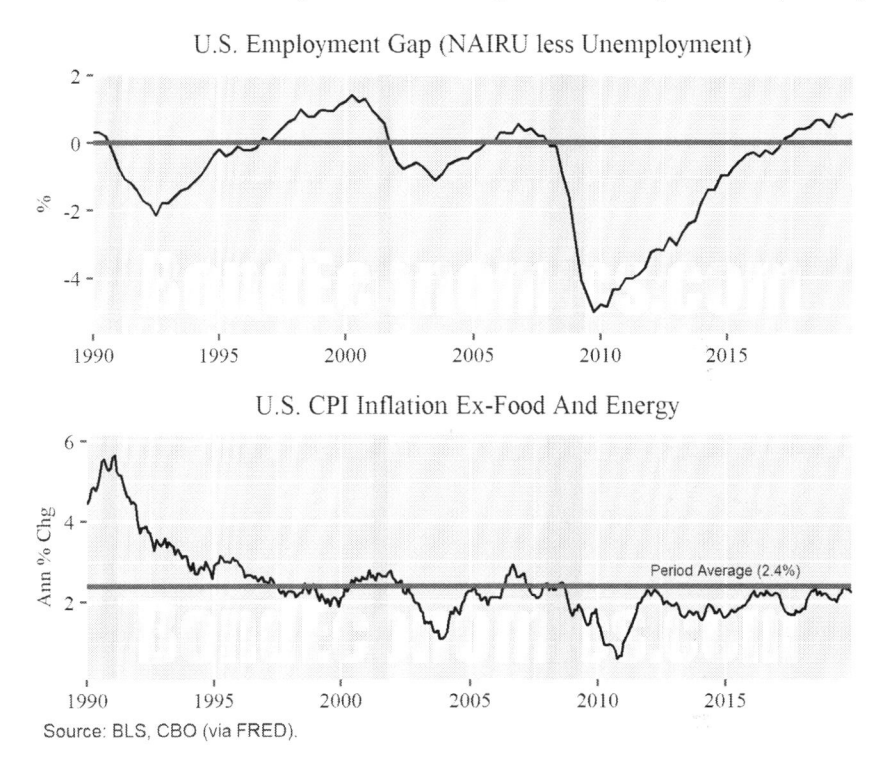

U.S. Employment Gap (NAIRU less Unemployment)

U.S. CPI Inflation Ex-Food And Energy

Period Average (2.4%)

Source: BLS, CBO (via FRED).

The figure above repeats the analysis with core consumer price inflation – excluding food and energy. (Although the use of core inflation distresses some people, the difference between headline and core is largely the result of gasoline prices. Energy prices are important, but oil price spikes cannot be exclusively pinned on U.S. domestic policy settings in the post-1990s period.

If we put aside the period of relatively high inflation in the early 1990s, we see that core CPI inflation stuck near its period average of 2.4% - with dips that occurred after the recessions that started in 2001 and 2008. Core CPI inflation was correlated with the employment gap – an unsurprising outcome given they are both pro-cyclical – but given the scale on the graph, we see that "acceleration" in inflation is negligible.

With some ingenuity, one could attempt to explain away the lack of acceleration by appealing to other factors that coincidentally always managed to cancel out the acceleration predicted by the NAIRU concept. I will return to that argument in the technical appendix.

The Policy Debates

The three expansions after 1990 featured the same debate: the unemployment rate is about to drop below NAIRU, so should the Federal Reserve hike rates to counteract the risks of rising inflation? The lack of accelerating inflation was typically seen as the result of flawed estimates of NAIRU; if we improved the methodology, NAIRU was lower than expected. Pavlina R. Tcherneva discusses the "search for NAIRU" in Chapter 2 of *The Case for a Job Guarantee*.

This argument that any particular NAIRU estimate (like the one produced by the CBO) is flawed and could be replaced by a better one is entirely reasonable. If we assume that economics is a science, we need to adapt our theories to observed data. However, I have some deep reservations with this view. Given the complexity of the topic, I have deferred this discussion to a technical appendix at the end of this section.

Rather than debate estimation methodologies, there is a much simpler alternative: NAIRU does not exist. The title of Chapter 4 of *Full Employment Abandoned*, "The troublesome NAIRU: the hoax that undermined full employment," offers a hint as to what the authors' views on the matter are.

From my experience, when one argues that NAIRU does not exist, one is hit with a wall of objections. The objections that I have seen were not particularly strong, as my feeling is that the people raising the objection are conflating "NAIRU does not exist" with "there is no relationship between unemployment and inflation."

I will start off stating what I see as a minimal version of the statement "NAIRU does not exist" – which is my construction. Once this logic is outlined, I will then discuss some of the comments from *Full Employment Abandoned*, which is an authoritative source for an MMT view.

I argue that the following terms are safe observations to make about the business cycle.
1. Inflation (however defined) is positively correlated with the business cycle: it tends to rise during an expansion.
2. The unemployment rate is negatively correlated with the business cycle. (Seems obvious, but people can enter/leave the workforce.)
3. The two previous statements imply that one should expect to see a local relationship between unemployment rate changes and the

inflation rate. This implies that we can typically fit a NAIRU-style relationship to a small segment of historical data.
4. The unemployment rate and annual (core) inflation both feature trending behaviour: the level in the current period is relatively close to historical values. (There is considerable noise in annualised inflation rates on a month-to-month basis, but that noise tends to cancel out, so that the annual average follows a trend.)
5. This trending behaviour means that the local models in (3) can be spliced together in back history, but one would expect that predictions based on such splices will tend to break down.

The implication of this logic is straightforward. It is a mistake to look at historical data and argue that if the unemployment rate drops below some arbitrary level in future years, inflation will accelerate. That was the mistake that policymakers and market participants kept making over the 1990-2020 period.

Mitchell and Muysken phrase the idea differently.

We have demonstrated (in Section 4.2) that contrary to theoretical claims of the natural rate theorists, non-structural variables have an impact on the NAIRU, which means that aggregate demand variations can alter the steady-state unemployment rate. This insight, alone, undermines the concept of natural unemployment, or NAIRU, which is driven by the notion that only structural measures can be taken if the government wants to reduce the current steady-state unemployment rate. As a consequence it is little wonder that the concept of equilibrium unemployment lost its original structural meaning and becomes indistinguishable in dynamics from the actual unemployment rate. [Section 4.2, page 116]

These statements are somewhat more complex than saying NAIRU does not exist, rather it is saying that if it existed, it does not behave the way that "natural rate theorists" suppose. I prefer the simplicity of the blunt version, but if one wants nuance, this is the version to use.

The jargon about "structural" and "non-structural" might be unfamiliar. "Structural" factors are institutional barriers that allegedly cause people to remain unemployed. From the neoliberal perspective, these are mainly the result of social programmes that give incomes to the unemployed. Non-structural factors are those related to the business cycle. I now will turn to one such factor that is highlighted by Mitchell and Muysken: hysteresis.

Hysteresis

Bill Mitchell's work in the 1980s emphasised the concept of *hysteresis*, although the idea has a longer history. (*Full Employment Abandoned* provides a 1972 quotation from Edmund Phelps that used the term in this context.) Hysteresis is a term used in physics and is typically described as "path dependence."

In the case of unemployment, the definition is as follows. Firstly, we need to assume that we can define something resembling NAIRU so that the employment gap offers useful predictions about inflation. If hysteresis is present, this measure is affected by the historical trajectory of unemployment. More specifically, if the rate of unemployment is high, the estimated "NAIRU" will rise.

Although this might sound like the case without hysteresis, this has radically different policy implications. By driving the unemployment rate lower, the value of "NAIRU" is lower. It implies that there can be a trade-off between unemployment and inflation, and that policies that create employment are optimal – since they are associated with lower steady state unemployment. Meanwhile, this helps explain the lack of inflation acceleration discussed earlier. If "NAIRU" is just tracking the unemployment rate (similar to taking a moving average), inflation will not move very much.

There are several ways in which hysteresis can arise – the literature surveyed in *Full Employment Abandoned* gives a number of mechanisms. Although this is of interest to academics, from a practical perspective it means that "NAIRU with hysteresis" does not behave the way the consensus assumes (e.g., the only way to lower it is through "structural reforms"). From a forecasting perspective, the resulting measure is largely useless. Since the reality is so far away from the conventional description of NAIRU, I would argue that the simplest description of the situation is that "NAIRU does not exist."

From the perspective of MMT, the key conclusion to draw from this line of argument is that it makes little sense to keep people unemployed in order to stabilise the price level. This will be expanded upon in the discussion of the Job Guarantee in Chapter 3.

Technical Appendix: Falsifiability?

Given that the neoclassical consensus decided that inflation control is the most important task for policy, it is no surprise that a great deal of effort has been expended upon the analysis of inflation. As such, just showing a couple time series plots is not the final word on this topic. Nevertheless, the outlook for NAIRU is not much better even if we dig deeper.

The first thing to realise is that we can very easily reject the belief that NAIRU is a constant, or that inflation depends solely upon the employment gap. We need a more complex model, where other factors influence inflation, and the estimate of NAIRU changes over time (as does the CBO series).

The addition of the extra factors gives the defenders of the concept of NAIRU (and its close cousins) an extra line of defense. Those other factors always managed to shift in such a fashion so that inflation did not accelerate, even with a non-zero employment gap. So, we can find a model that has a good fit to the back history.

Unfortunately, there are two explanations for this.

1. The more complex model is correct.
2. The model is wrong, and the employment gap does not cause inflation to accelerate.

Since central bankers and academics are paid to produce models that predict economic outcomes, it is perhaps unsurprising that the first option was chosen, and the second brushed aside.

Neoclassical theory is highly dependent upon variables that are inferred from the data:

- the natural rate of unemployment/NAIRU;
- potential GDP (a replacement to the above);
- the natural rate of interest (r^*).

Economic outcomes are the result of observed variables (unemployment, GDP, interest rates) from these theoretical constructs. Since the variables cannot be directly measured, they are inferred from statistical procedures *that assume that the underlying neoclassical theory is correct*.

Neoclassical theorists have little difficulty believing that the underlying assumptions of their theories are correct. However, outsiders have good cause to question the falsifiability of the methodology. Since the level of the hidden variables is backed out from observed data, there is no way that historical data can deviate from the model predictions.

However, we are not interested in predicting historical events, we need forward-looking behaviour. As one might suspect, the models do a decent job in fitting economic data following smooth trends, but have a hard time dealing with turning points (mainly recessions, which is a sub-theme of my text *Recessions*). Longer-term extrapolations – such as inflation rising when NAIRU is hit in future years – also fail, with the failure covered up by continuous cuts to the estimated value of NAIRU.

To give a somewhat concrete example of falsifiability with respect to r^*, imagine that the estimated value of r^* is 1% ahead of recession. The central bank cuts rates to 0%, inflation is stable at 2% (implying a -2% policy rate), yet the economy does not accelerate. The estimation technique used to update the estimate of r^* will note the lack of acceleration in the economy, and so revise down its estimate of r*. If the variables do not move, the r^* estimate will keep getting revised lower, until the estimate converges with -2%. Since the real policy rate has converged to the r^* estimate, the model will then be able to explain the lack of acceleration. (One may note that this scenario overlaps the post-2008 history, albeit simplified.)

However, the exact same outcome could result in an economic model that suggests that the real policy rate has zero effect on the economy, and so may do just as good a job as explaining observed data. If the statistical procedure cannot distinguish between the possibilities that interest rates either affect the economy or they do not, the premise is unfalsifiable.

My comments here seem to be consistent with post-Keynesian discussion of the subject, but perhaps with different wording. It should be noted that not only post-Keynesians have raised this critique, Roger E. Farmer made the same argument about falsifiability in Chapter 3 of *Prosperity for All: How to Prevent Financial Crises*. He summarises his argument as:

> But, I am unaware of any theory that provides us in advance with an explanation of how the natural rate of unemployment varies over time. In the absence of such a theory, the NRH has no predictive content. A theory like this -- which cannot be falsified by any set of observations – is religion, not science.

References and Further Reading

- *Full Employment Abandoned: Shifting Sands and Policy Failures*, William Mitchell and Joan Muysken, Edward Elgar Publishing, 2008. ISBN: 978-1-85898-507-7
- *The Case for a Job Guarantee,* Pavlina R. Tcherneva, Polity Press, 2020. ISBN: 978-1-5095-4211-6
- *Unemployment: Macroeconomic Performance and the Labour Market*, by Layard, Nickell, and Jackman, 1991, Oxford University Press. (This text was influential in setting the European mainstream consensus on la-

bour market policy.)
- *Prosperity for All: How to Prevent Financial Crises.* Roger E. A. Farmer, Oxford University Press, 2017. ISBN: 9780190621438.

2.4 The Drift to Austerity

Debates about fiscal policy and government debt are arguably what created most of the publicity for Modern Monetary Theory. After the Financial Crisis of 2008, government debt-to-GDP ratios rose, which was a greater concern in the euro area as there was a limit on that ratio within the Maastricht treaty. At the same time, there was popular anger at bank bailouts across the political spectrum – bankers caused the crisis, and then were bailed out by governments. This free-floating anger attached to worries about government debt. As a result, governments implemented austerity packages, which typically consisted of cutting spending on social welfare programmes.

Although this debate helps explain the rise of MMT, one could argue that the consensus has drifted in the direction of MMT. Moreover, the fact that MMT proponents have been pushing for looser fiscal policy for some time is well known. As such, I am keeping this treatment relatively brief.

The MMT View of Austerity

Worrying about fiscal deficits or the level of governmental debt runs directly counter to the principles of Functional Finance, which lie within *narrow MMT*. As a result, the popular debates about austerity cemented the importance of narrow MMT with respect to the theoretical project.

For a country with adequate control of its currency (commonly referred to as *currency sovereignty*), there is no economic force that can cause it to "run out of money." At most, the central government can run into self-imposed constraints, like the ridiculous American Debt Ceiling Fiasco of 2013. Such a government effectively cannot be forced to default (unlike users of the currency), and even the interest rate paid on government debt is a policy variable. (The argument that nominal bond yields are under the government's control is strongly disputed by others, but the rise of the concept of Yield Curve Control has shown that such objections are on extremely shaky ground, even from a mainstream perspective.)

An important qualification of the previous statements is that a country has a strong level of currency sovereignty. Although some countries are clearly not currency sovereigns – countries that borrow in a foreign currency or peg the value of their currency – other countries lie on a currency sovereignty spectrum. The non-euro developed countries have a high level of currency sovereignty, while many developing countries are in a position where they are extremely sensitive to global capital markets. Many critics of MMT have an exaggerated view of dependence upon capital markets, and often make assertions that only the United States has such sovereignty. This ignores the reality that Canada – with a relatively small economy that is wide open to foreign trade – has floated its currency for almost all the post-1950 period.

To be fair, some people could dispute that assessment, raising the alleged fiscal crisis in Canada in the early 1990s, in which "twin deficits" supposedly forced a fiscal retrenchment. I do not want to pursue that argument, but I would note that only evidence that a crisis happened is almost entirely anecdotal – it is based on the opinions of economists, many of whom wanted Canada to slash the size of the state. (One may note that economists were generally not reliable in this respect, the consensus spent most of the post-1995 period worried about a fiscal crisis in Japan.) On the contrary side, it is almost impossible to detect a fiscal crisis in secondary bond market yields. If bond investors expected a default, there would be extreme price movements to compensate for expected losses. What is less open to dispute is that Canada had relatively high inflation, driven by Old Keynesian policies, and the fiscal retrenchment arguably was a factor behind inflation stability. However, tightening fiscal policy to reduce inflationary pressures is not equivalent to being on the verge of default due to bond or foreign exchange vigilantes.

Other developed countries caught up to Canada's free-floating approach, starting with the demise of the Bretton Woods system in the 1970s, but some clung to pegged systems (such as the U.K.'s membership in the European Exchange Rate Mechanism before its ejection in 1992).

Although there was no economic logic behind austerity, it was politically attractive to its proponents. It allowed governments to cut social welfare spending, while being able to claim that "bond markets" forced the spending cuts.

Stephanie Kelton outlined the myths that led to the austerity campaign in her best-selling book, *The Deficit Myth*. They are listed below (with a few wording tweaks to eliminate American-specific terms and switching to Canadian spelling); I refer the reader to *The Deficit Myth* for more details.

1. Myth: A currency sovereign should budget like a household. Reality: Unlike a household, a currency sovereign issues the cur-

rency it spends.
2. Myth: Deficits are evidence of overspending. Reality: For evidence of overspending, look to inflation.
3. Myth: One way or another, we're all on the hook for government debt. Reality: The national debt poses no financial burden whatsoever.
4. Myth: Government deficits crowd out private investment, making us poorer. Reality: Fiscal deficits increase our wealth and collective savings.
5. Myth: The trade deficit means America is losing. America's trade deficit is its "stuff" surplus.
6. Myth: "Entitlement" programmes like Social Security and Medicare are financially unsustainable. We can't afford them anymore. Reality: As long as the central government commits to making the payments, it can always afford to support these programmes. What matters is our economy's long-run capacity to produce the real goods and services people need.

At present, it is easy to find mainstream (or heterodox) economists that argue that MMT's views on fiscal policy are not particularly novel. However, this glosses over the reality that the myths referred to by Kelton were being propagated by neoclassical economists for decades. Even if a particular mainstream economist did not subscribe to the myths, other high-profile ones did. The myths outlined by Kelton were arguably consensus views (although this is less true in 2020).

The Effects of Austerity

The dismal policy failures after the Financial Crisis were where views on fiscal policy were most obviously negative for growth. The poster child for disastrous policy was in the Euro periphery, as seen in the collapse of Greek nominal GDP (next figure). Such a contraction in GDP in a developed country with a welfare state was largely thought to be impossible, yet the brain trust in Europe managed that feat. Hyman Minsky wrote an essay "Can 'It' Happen Again?" (with "It" referring to a depression), and he argued that the modern welfare state made such contractions less likely.

Greek Nominal GDP

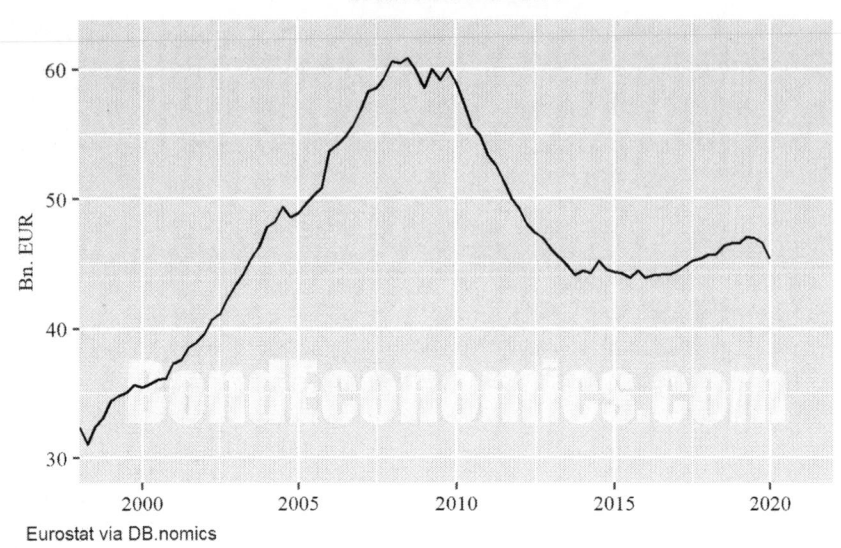

Eurostat via DB.nomics

The nature of the euro (an internal currency peg system) made Greece's fate inevitable given the disregard for the welfare of Greek citizens shown by the euro area authorities. Greece is not a currency sovereign, and so either had to knuckle under to the Troika, or somehow leave the euro. (The euro was designed to make exit extremely painful.) However, even floating currency sovereigns hopped onto the austerity bandwagon for political reasons. Arguing that their country "would become the next Greece," was an easy way to sell policies that would have otherwise been more unpopular – mainly slashing social safety net spending. These cuts came after the end of the recession and helped bake in low growth rates.

Even the leading currency sovereign – the United States – was not immune to policymakers that refused to take fiscal policy seriously. In the introduction to *The Deficit Myth*, Stephanie Kelton describes the Obama administration response to the crisis as follows.

> She [Economist Christina Romer] had run the numbers, and she concluded that a package as large as $1.8 trillion might be required to combat the worsening situation. But that option was nixed by Lawrence Summers, the Harvard economist and former treasury secretary who became Obama's chief economic advisor. Summers might have preferred a bigger stimulus, but he worried that asking Congress for anything close to $1 trillion would provoke ridicule, saying that "the public wouldn't stand for it, and it would never get through Congress."

Canadian General Government Expenditures

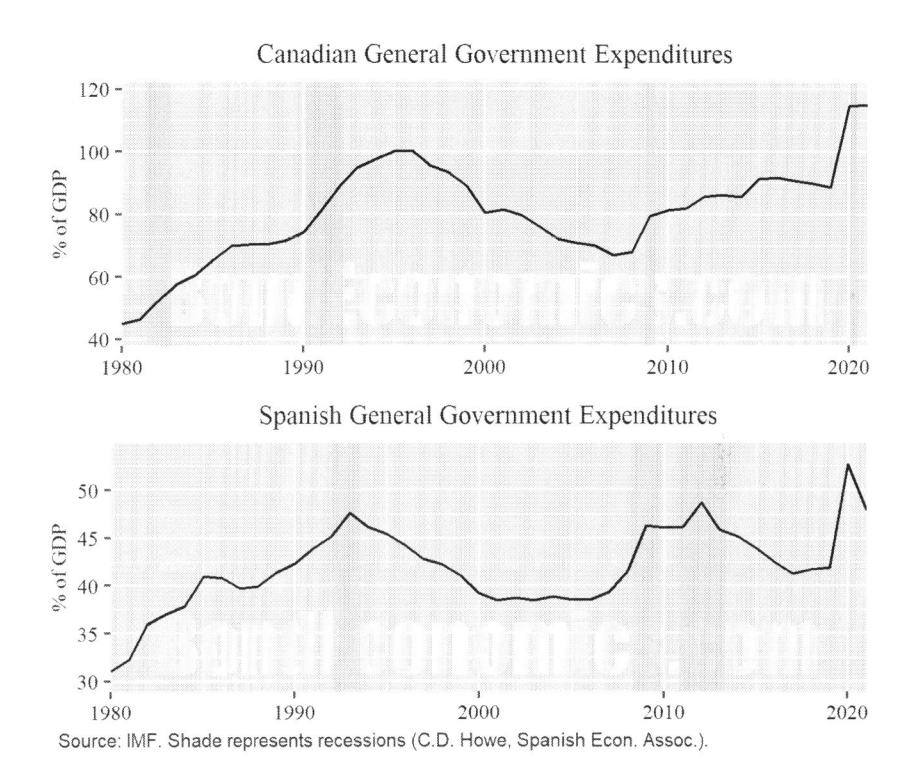

Spanish General Government Expenditures

Source: IMF. Shade represents recessions (C.D. Howe, Spanish Econ. Assoc.).

However, austerity policies were not only a factor in the post-Financial Crisis period. In addition to labour market reforms, the 1990s saw a shrinking of the government sector. The chart above shows two well-known examples, Canada and Spain. It was not purely a question of the role of government shrinking, the mix of spending changed. As became apparent in 2020, very few expenses have been spared in equipping the police or the military. The political reality in the United States is that "military Keynesianism" is the bipartisan consensus method to create government jobs. The problem is that military equipment is now highly advanced, and so the spending creates a relatively small number of highly paid jobs. Although creating jobs with high pay sounds attractive, this does little for people caught in under-employment, and it creates inflationary pressures in affected occupations (e.g., electrical engineers).

Bidding up wages in occupations already facing capacity constraints was the Achilles heel of hydraulic Keynesianism, and the theoretical focus on aggregates means that this theoretical blind spot remains. Although MMT critics accuse MMTers of being cheerleaders of government spending, the reality is that MMT is focussed on *how* governments spend.

Will This Time Be Different?

Will there be an austerity backlash in the coming years, citing the rise in government debt-to-GDP ratios? (At the time of writing, those ratios have not yet stabilised, but it seems safe to predict that they will approach peacetime, if not wartime, records.)

It is a very safe bet that free market-oriented parties will make austerity politics a plank in their campaigns. Historically, conservative parties had factions that could accept Keynesian economics – e.g., country club Republicans, the Tory Wets in the U.K., and the Red Tories in Canada – but those are now an endangered (if not extinct) species. That said, politicians have some instinct for self-preservation, and are unlikely to want to push the economy into a deep recession voluntarily. (The European authorities were able to do this after the Financial Crisis because foreigners were the ones disciplining the periphery; they did not have to face peripheral voters to keep their jobs.) Admittedly, Republican politicians appear to be swinging towards embracing austerity in order to undermine the Biden administration, but this may be in the context of an expansion. In any event, no matter what the details of the debates are, the reality is that social programmes have already been cut in previous decades. Just preserving the *status quo* is enough to ensure that fiscal policy will only act to blunt the worst of the recession, but not be vigorous enough to rapidly reduce the unemployment rate in steady state.

From the perspective of economic theory, the failures of austerity policies in the last cycle seem to be well understood enough that the debate may be the arcane "how is MMT different from neoclassical economics?" (although free market-oriented economists will find reasons to support tighter fiscal policy). This may be more boring than the economic debates in the 2010s, since they might split purely on partisan lines. For the debates to have substantive value, they will need to be in reference to discussing the details of actual programmes. That said, Canada is in a position where many in the ruling elites have not updated their views since the early 1990s, and so the debate will resemble the ones seen a decade earlier.

References and Further Reading

- *The Deficit Myth: Modern Monetary Theory and the Birth of the People's Economy*, by Stephanie Kelton. PublicAffairs, Hachette Book Group, 2020. ISBN: 978-1-5417-3618-4

- *Can "It" Happen Again?: Essay On Instability and Finance,* by Hyman P. Minsky. M.E. Sharpe, Inc., 1982. ISBN: 0-87332-213-4

2.5 The Rise and Decline of Inflation Targeting

From the perspective of economic theory, the gap between the view of Modern Monetary Theory and conventional economics with regard to monetary policy is the starkest difference. If we look at the views before the Financial Crisis, it is only a slight exaggeration to say that neoclassical economists put almost all their weight behind the use of monetary policy and avoided fiscal policy, while MMTers took exactly the opposite approach.

That said, the difference has faded courtesy of policy rates smashing into what was known as the Zero Lower Bound (ZLB) for interest rates. Since some regions have experimented with slightly negative interest rates, this is better thought of as the Effective Lower Bound (ELB). Since conventional interest rate policy hit a limit, central banks have experimented with unconventional policies (e.g., negative policy rates, quantitative easing (QE)). This reality has reasonably dampened the enthusiasm for monetary policy, and so there has been a movement towards the MMT stance (albeit for different reasons).

I want to emphasise that this is a primer about MMT, not neoclassical economics. A good deal of discussion in this section references neoclassical thinking. I aim to present the neoclassical ideas in a good faith fashion, but I have strong reservations about them. The safest option is to offer a simplified outline of ideas, and not spend time detailing an incompatible theory. Another thing to keep in mind is that the post-Keynesian/MMT academic literature has spent considerable time attacking the inflation-targeting obsession of earlier decades, and so the available critiques are far more detailed than the outline here.

Inflation Targeting

U.S. Core CPI Inflation

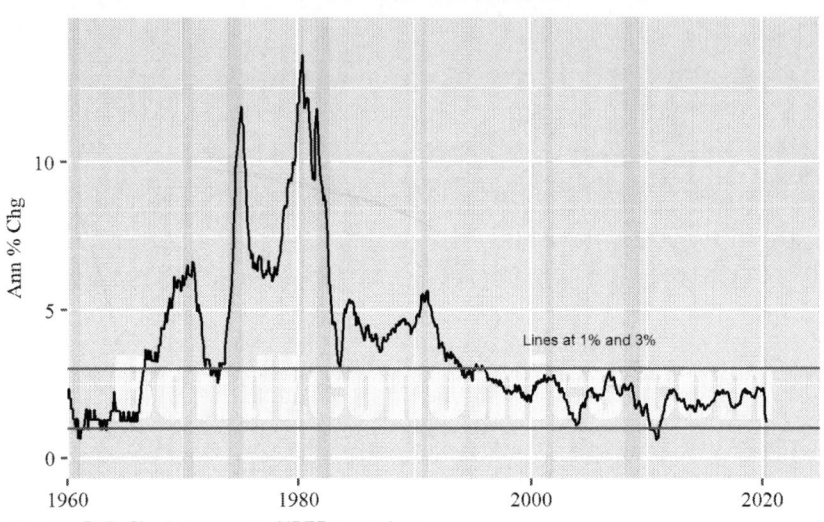

Source: BLS. Shade represents NBER recessions.

The consensus mainstream reaction to relatively high inflation during the 1970s was to endorse the concept of inflation targeting. The argument was that the central bank needs to be made "independent," and it should have one primary objective – to keep inflation near a target level. This theoretical consensus made its way to central banks, and New Zealand was the first country to adopt this framework in 1990. It was followed by other countries. The U.S. did not formally adopt inflation targeting (it has a wider formal mandate), but the popular argument is that the Federal Reserve has been a *de facto* inflation targeting bank since the early 1990s. As the chart above shows, U.S. core CPI inflation (core means excluding energy and food) has largely been confined to the 1%-3% range since the early 1990s. If one includes energy prices, various oil price spikes have caused greater volatility in all items ("headline") CPI, but these price rises/falls were not persistent (and did not drag the rest of the price index along for the ride).

It should be noted that inflation stability was not a U.S.-specific phenomenon. The inflation rates for most developed countries looked like the above chart over the 1990-2008 period, albeit with the occasional spike in data. There is a pair of notable exceptions. The first is Japan, where price changes bounced around the 0% level, rather than a positive average.

The other exceptions were in the euro periphery in the aftermath of the Financial Crisis, where austerity-driven depressions were more disruptive.

Central bankers obviously would like to claim credit for the stability of the inflation rate since the early 1990s. Meanwhile, proponents of MMT would likely argue that inflation stability over that era is tied to labour market reforms – which were also implemented in the early 1990s (Section 2.2). Meanwhile, fiscal policy was tightened, as seen in the Canadian and Spanish government spending charts shown in Section 2.4. As will be discussed below, this is an intricate debate.

Monetary Policy Dominance

An idea related to inflation targeting is monetary dominance. The consensus view in neoclassical economics was that an independent central bank will act to cancel out any attempt by the fiscal authorities to stimulate the economy. As such, only monetary policy should be used to moderate the economic cycle; the fiscal arm of government is supposed to stay out of the way. This fit into the neoliberal policy consensus perfectly.

(As a technical note, some economists of the monetarist persuasion argue that monetary policy is not the use of interest rates to steer the economy, rather the central bank controls money supply growth. This is not widely accepted, but I note it because some readers may be familiar with this characterisation.)

One of the defining characteristics of post-Keynesian economics is that the neoclassical emphasis on monetary policy is misguided. However, the level of disagreement falls on a spectrum, with MMT proponents generally the most skeptical.

Variants of Skepticism

The least common denominator of the post-Keynesian skepticism is that the effects of interest rate changes are mixed, and the mainstream consensus about the drawbacks of fiscal policy stabilisation are overstated. Saying that effects are "mixed" appears to be a consensus way of describing the MMT position, although this masks a mild divergence of views.

A stronger version of skepticism is that interest rate changes have negligible effects on the economy – possibly outside of certain circumstances. As an example of such circumstances one might accept that rapid rate rises can destabilise a highly indebted private sector, triggering a recession. (This is my view, and I do not have reason to believe that too many people will violently disagree with this.) A related extension is that housing markets are typically sensitive to interest rates, even in the absence of a crisis. Given the importance of housing bubbles in recent decades in driving growth, this is not a minor technical issue.

The reasons to be skeptical about the effect of interest rate policy are that there is no belief that they moderate behaviour in the way that is assumed in neoclassical macro. Fixed investment is a major driver of the economic cycle, and investment decisions appear to be more sensitive to the prospects for demand than interest rates. (As a result of the usual reaction function of central banks, interest rates and fixed investment peak at the same time since they are both pro-cyclical variables.)

The most extreme skepticism comes in the form of the argument that interest rate changes generally work in exactly the opposite way predicted by neoclassicals: raising interest rates *raises* inflation. There are two legs to this argument: rising interest rates on government debt act as a form of fiscal stimulus. The other leg is that interest is a cost of doing business, and so it is embedded in sales prices. Within MMT, Warren Mosler is one of the more outspoken proponents of the view that neoclassicals are looking at interest rate policy backwards (although his *White Paper* hedges this with a "may" – Section 4.2). Although an uncommon view now, based on my reading of archived financial market commentary, "raising interest raises inflation" appeared quite often in 1970s market analysis, although it may have been disreputable with academics. (This possibility does appear within mainstream discussions of "fiscal dominance," but this possibility is normally brushed aside; "fiscal dominance" somehow just pops into existence based on some vaguely-defined threshold.)

(As a technical note, there is a faction within neoclassical economics – the *Neo-Ricardians* – who also assert that the standard view of interest rate policy is backwards.)

Divide Not Easily Bridged

Beliefs about how monetary policy works are the consensus within financial markets. So much so that I did not see the need to explain what they are earlier. (For completeness, cutting interest rates stimulates growth and inflation, while raising rates slows growth and inflation. Technically, the real rate of interest is what is looked at, but in the modern era, nominal rates move faster than inflation, so the movements are directionally similar.)

I would have expected the MMT/post-Keynesian skepticism about this would attract more attention; but I was clearly wrong. Even though this stance is critical in understanding MMT discussion of policy, it is ignored in favour of scare stories about "money printing," which end up being rather boring once one understands the MMT stance. Financial market participants have become obsessed with central bank activity, and the possibility that monetary policy is ineffective is so far off the radar that it does not even register.

Meanwhile, the belief that monetary policy is ineffective (or backwards!) is one that is designed to kill a career in a central bank.

If we step beyond the psychological aspects of this divide, we see that it matters a lot for policy discussions. *Most critiques of MMT just assume that the conventional story about interest rate policy is true.* It goes without saying that if you assume a contested point is true, it looks like you win the argument. The issue is that it needs to be demonstrated that MMT proponents are wrong about interest rate policy. I see no conclusive evidence – either way.

ZLB'd

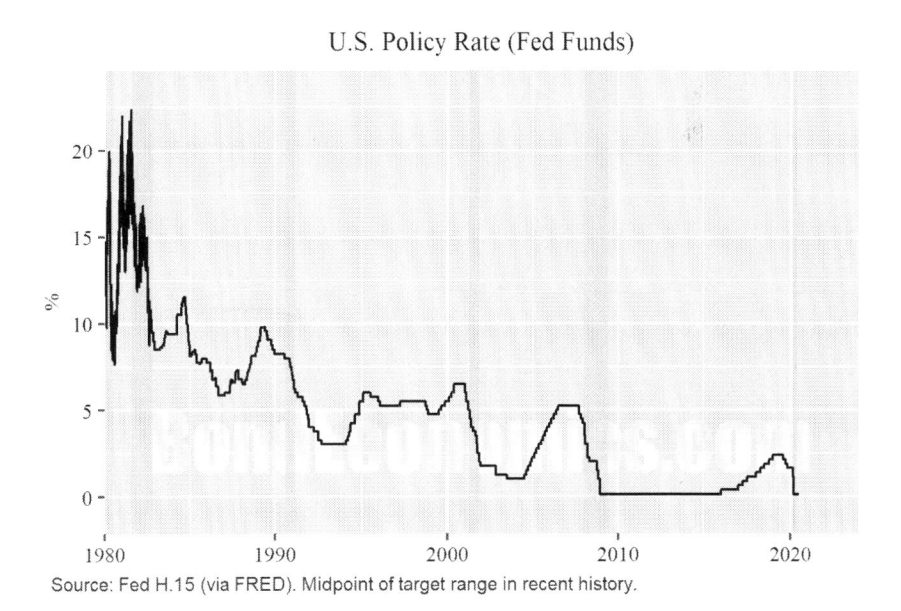

U.S. Policy Rate (Fed Funds)

Source: Fed H.15 (via FRED). Midpoint of target range in recent history.

As noted earlier, reality has interfered with the neoclassical narrative. As the chart above shows, the policy rate has marched lower since the early 1980s interest rate insanity. The peak interest rate in each cycle has gotten lower, while the bottom has crashed into 0%. Although other jurisdictions have experimented with negative policy rates, the Federal Reserve has held off – for now.

One may note that the above picture is exactly what one would predict if fiscal and labour market policy skewed the economy towards low growth, and low interest rates are not particularly stimulative for growth ("pushing on a string").

As such, the current policy debate has swung closer to the MMT view: conventional interest rate policy is no longer effective *at present*. It might not be a consensus view yet – various economists are holding out for various unconventional versions of monetary policy – but the stance is certainly no longer surprising. The controversy returns when discussing scenarios where inflation and interest rates are rising. As such, the debate is just paused until interest rates rise.

Could "unconventional" monetary policy kick the economy back into growth? It seems clear that Quantitative Easing is largely pointless – it largely just gave hard money proponents a chance to embarrass themselves by making hyperinflation forecasts. However, other unconventional "monetary" policies that are just disguised fiscal policy could generate some growth. However, this is a question of semantics and politics (should politicians hand over the power of the purse to unelected bureaucrats?).

References and Further Reading

The commentary in this section largely represents my views on this subject. Given my background as a rates analyst, I have my own preferred way of describing this topic. There is a vast neoclassical literature on inflation targeting, as well as new proposals to overcome some defects.

The following reference is close to the subject matter of this section. Otherwise, one would need to delve into the MMT/post-Keynesian literature to examine their analysis of interest rate policy, and the discussion will typically go in a different direction.

- There is a discussion of the shift to inflation targeting in Chapter 6 of *Full Employment Abandoned: Shifting Sands and Policy Failures*, William Mitchell and Joan Muysken, Edward Elgar Publishing, 2008. ISBN: 978-1-85898-507-7

Chapter 3 Doing Better

3.1 Introduction

Having outlined why economies have been stuck in a low-growth rut, we now switch to discussing what might cause growth to perk up.

The emphasis on labour markets in the previous chapter indicates to us where trends need to change. Although one might hope that some private sector boom tightens up the labour market as a result of market forces, the track record suggests that we will need policy shifts to push the economy in that direction.

This chapter outlines major reforms suggested by MMT proponents, mainly the Job Guarantee and the Green New Deal. The Job Guarantee is aimed directly at the underemployment problem and provides a workforce for parts of the Green New Deal. The Green New Deal is put forth as an ambitious set of programmes to re-orient society away from carbon emissions. This restricting implies a need for a renewed push in fixed investment, ending the problem of underemployment, flipping the concern to managing a high-pressure economy.

Since this book is oriented around MMT, some reforms to government finance are discussed. They would not magically improve growth themselves, rather they would prevent errors created by incompetent analysis. At the time of writing, fiscal conservatives are recovering from the shock of the pandemic crisis, and are spinning new yarns about fiscal sustainability.

3.2 Fiscal Policy Reform

Most discussions about MMT revolve around fiscal policy. The first thing to keep in mind is that MMT proponents argue that the framework for analysing fiscal policy needs to be changed. The title of the article "[Replacing the Budget Constraint with an Inflation Constraint](#)" by Scott Fullwiler summarises the change perfectly.

Functional Finance suggests that inflation constrains fiscal policy for a floating currency sovereign, not financing concerns. As such, that is how budgets ought to be analysed.

This is a non-trivial change, and given the difficulty of modelling inflation, people will disagree over details. Nevertheless, it is better to attempt the correct thing rather than do the wrong thing because it is easier.

Another reason to emphasise this topic is that it nullifies a significant portion of MMT criticism (which we will wade into in Chapter 5). The premise of MMT fiscal policy analysis is that the effect on inflation is the correct methodology. By implication, it makes no sense to complain that "implementing MMT" is somehow inflationary by itself. (Variations of that wording are extremely common in internet discussions.) The only way that critique makes sense is that the critic and MMT proponent analyse inflation risks differently. That is entirely possible, so the criticism cannot be completely ignored. That said, we need to look at the competing methods of analysing inflation, and most critics do not take that extra step.

Fullwiler Article

The Fullwiler article was in response to analysis by Tim Worstall. The following text summarises the argument.

> As argued bazillions of times, the real point MMT is making is that the government's budget constraint is the wrong constraint—the correct constraint is whether or not a particular budget position will raise inflation beyond an official target rate (say, 2%, which seems to be the choice of most central bankers).
>
> Let me explain to Mr. Worstall and others how this could work rather easily—just as the CBO and OMB now evaluate government budget proposals regarding their effects on the budget stance, the CBO and OMB could instead shift focus on evaluating these proposals against the inflation target (I argued the same thing here [link to SSRN paper]). Much like how policy makers supposedly take estimates of effects on the budget position rather seriously in making budget conditions, they could replace these with projections of inflationary effects. An inflation constraint provides more fiscal space than a budget constraint, but in no way does it provide unlimited fiscal space (again, as we've always argued).

Fullwiler notes that expertise to do such functional finance analysis has withered. This was a feature of wartime planning, but discouraged by the consensus.

Difficulties

Although it seems clear that *excessively* loose fiscal policy poses inflation risks in the absence of demand management policies that were implemented in World War II, drawing the line where "excessive" starts is not at all obvious. If we look at the post-1990 policy environment, we see that no implemented policies caused a large deviation from inflation target levels (Section 2.5).

Therefore, under current institutional conditions, there is clearly a buffer area where fiscal policy changes do not have a measurable effect on inflationary outcomes. There are many competing explanations for this possibility, and I would argue that not everyone agrees on which one(s) are correct.

Another thing to keep in mind is that observed outcomes are the result of decision-making in both the private and public sectors. If the private sector launches a delusional fixed investment bubble, it can cause observed inflation to rise above target – even if governmental policy in the absence of the bubble left inflation on target. *All forecasting approaches must contend with fundamental uncertainty.*

The post-Keynesian theory of inflation suggests that it is a far more complex process than suggested by aggregated neoclassical models. I do not expect that it will be easy to write down an abstract approach to Functional Finance that will work under all circumstances.

Another practical issue is that each government approaches this task differently. The American budget process is convoluted and reforming it from within is extremely difficult. Conversely, a country with a powerful executive (e.g., the Prime Minister's Office in Canada) might be able to push a change through, and let the civil service deal with the complications.

Factors in Favour of the Approach

Although I agree that an abstract approach to Functional Finance that applies to *any* budgeting situation is an extremely complex task, the government has the means to make its life less difficult. In particular, it does not need to be price taker (Section 4.3). A major reason why the Old Keynesians helped drive the inflationary cycle was that they wasted efforts on aggregated analysis, and they did not understand the causes of inflationary pressure. Modern neoclassicals follow the same aggregated approach, and based on comments by critics, they assume that MMT proponents do the same.

If we look at the *Monetary Monopoly Model* discussed in Chapter 4, we see that the government can fix the price it is willing to pay for goods and services, and let the quantities adjust. To a certain extent, this is partly done: salaries and transfers are set as nominal quantities, although there is often (partial) indexation of these payments.

The idea is that the government needs to set the price it is willing to pay in other contexts. That is a key feature of the Job Guarantee (Section 3.3) – which explains why people like myself are not concerned about the long-term inflationary effect of the policy without even needing to dig into budget methodologies.

This principle can be extended, and departmental budgets could be set with conditions on prices paid. There will obviously be cases where the government will have no choice to be a price taker (e.g., imported equipment), but given that wages are a major part of expenditures, these expenses may not be too significant a portion of the budget.

Most of the time, governments are not making radical changes to their expenditure patterns. It seems very likely that back-of-the-envelope analyses will give adequate results for mild fiscal policy changes.

For larger changes, governments will need to dig into the real resource requirements of the policy, such as the materials used as well as personnel requirements. It is hard to set out the exact parameters of such an analysis that covers all possible policies; realistically, each programme needs to be judged on its own merits.

Another approach to deal with the inflationary aspects of governmental policy is to use administrative measures to control inflation. That is a controversial subject, and discussed in Section 5.6.

Concluding Remarks

The real concern about the side effects of fiscal policy changes is the effect on inflation. The fact that "hyperinflation" appears in most conventional criticism of MMT shows that this is a consensus view. Meanwhile, analysing inflation risks is difficult, and anyone offering a magic analytical solution – like the Friedman $k\%$ rule – is most likely incorrect. This is where policy debates ought to focus, instead of juvenile musings about "bond vigilantes."

Chapter 5 digs into criticism of MMT. Although I am not impressed with almost all of the critiques I outlined, I want to emphasise that getting inflationary analysis correct is non-trivial. As such, I am perfectly willing to accept that a particular inflation analysis by an MMT proponent is incorrect. That said, the MMT proponent will correctly be focussing on what matters – which cannot be said of many conventional analyses.

References and Further Reading

- "Replacing the Budget Constraint with an Inflation Constraint," by Scott Fullwiler. *New Economic Perspectives*, January 12, 2015. URL: https://neweconomicperspectives.org/2015/01/replacing-bud-

get-constraint-inflation-constraint.html
- "Functional Finance and the Debt Ratio" by Scott Fullwiler, January 4, 2013. URL: https://papers.ssrn.com/sol3/papers.cfm?abstract_id=2196482

3.3 The Job Guarantee

The Job Guarantee is a programme that offers all citizens willing to work for it a guaranteed wage – which becomes the *de facto* minimum wage in the economy. It creates a floor for incomes and working conditions. It also gives the government a workforce that can undertake non-time sensitive projects. (Permanent government jobs would be unaffected.) The implementation of the programme would be country-specific, as the objective would be to re-use existing job seeking infrastructure. The central government would pay the workers and oversee the programme, but local governments and non-profits would likely be the employers, at least in larger countries.

The Job Guarantee is a core part of Modern Monetary Theory, both as a policy recommendation, as well from a theoretical perspective. The realisation that governments can use the pool of labour within the Job Guarantee programme in a fashion analogous to a commodity price support programme to stabilise the price level was independently observed by Warren Mosler and Bill Mitchell.

My description of the Job Guarantee leans heavily on *The Case for a Job Guarantee*, by Pavlina R. Tcherneva. That book describes the programme, as well as outlining the research behind it. I make some editorial comments, which does not necessarily align with Tcherneva's views, but those digressions are noted. Since most internet commentary from critics is concentrated on implementation difficulty, that is the focus herein.

Implementation Outline

The underlying premise of a Job Guarantee is that the central government guarantees that a job exists for all citizens willing to work at a fixed wage. Beyond that, the implementation could vary widely, and different authors might have different suggestions.

Pavlina Tcherneva argues that the best strategy is to not reinvent the wheel; existing programmes can be repurposed to fit within the Job Guarantee. In the United States, in addition to existing job centres, state and municipal governments already have job creation programmes, and non-profits are already recognised and "regulated" (their activities have to be certified by tax authorities). Meanwhile, these activities are typically under-funded and under-staffed.

The ease of implementation is going to be related to cyclical conditions. During the worst of the pandemic, it was difficult to organise new activities (given the unfamiliar physical distancing rules), and the number of potential entrants would have been extremely large. Conversely, the number of potential applicants would presumably be reasonable if the economy had been expanding for some time.

One common discussion point is whether these are really jobs, and whether people can be fired from them. Planting trees or cooking in a homeless shelter are certainly real jobs. Disruptive workers can be fired from the Job Guarantee, and they will end up on last chance social welfare programmes. (Since hardship cases of sick or disabled individuals will exist, such a safety net is still needed.) The guarantee is a job for people willing to work and is not an income guarantee.

With the exception of some youth apprenticeship programmes, the workers would not be made available to for-profit firms. Presumably, other training or education programmes would be coordinated with the Job Guarantee, but the details would vary widely by jurisdiction.

Tcherneva pointed out that governments already run some complex activities, such as kindergarten to high school in North America, or significant portions of health care outside of the United States. Shying away from manageable complexity is a defeatist attitude.

Benefits

I will keep the discussion of benefits brief, on the basis that most reasonable people understand that this programme benefits workers, their concern revolves around the costs/side-effects of the programme. I summarise some of the benefits as follows.
- A powerful automatic stabiliser and acts to stabilise inflation (unlike many alternatives).
- Unlike Old and New Keynesian aggregate-demand approaches, the spending is flowing exactly to the areas where demand is weak. By contrast, lowering interest rates helps fuel a property bubble in the big cities, while rural areas stagnate in poverty.
- Having people socialising in a workplace rather than being isolated

at home is advantageous.
- Society pays other costs associated with unemployment, and the existence of the programme would reduce them.
- Employers do not like hiring the long-term unemployed, as their "attachment to the workplace" is lost over time (e.g., habits like punctuality, or conformity to the social hierarchy from the perspective of an anarchist). Savvy employers that pay relatively low wages will develop relations with supervisors inside the programme (such as volunteers at non-profits) to get an honest appraisal of workers' abilities. (Warren Mosler emphasises this point, referring to the Job Guarantee as a "transition job.")
- The state has labour power to undertake non-time sensitive projects, such as long-term environmental remediation.
- The authorities have a new policy lever that allows them to influence wage differentials. (Some might view this as a negative.)

Steady State Inflation Stabilisation...
The basic assumption of analysis is that private sector firms will generally need to offer compensation that is at a premium to the Job Guarantee compensation package – or at least offer starting-level positions that offer the possibility of a promotion to better-compensated jobs. (Intern positions already draw in students at below-market pay as a way of getting office experience.)

Note that I wrote "compensation" in the previous paragraph, as the Job Guarantee could have benefits (like medical insurance or daycare) that are not already mandated/provided by the state. For simplicity in the rest of this text, I will refer to the wage differential between the Job Guarantee and private sector jobs, embedding other aspects of compensation into wages. This matches the terminology of conventional economic models, which use "wages" instead of "compensation" when modelling the labour market. The difference between wages and compensation is probably the most pronounced in the United States, which unusually lacks some form of socialised medical care – which implies that medical insurance is an important (and expensive) part of compensation. Since non-wage benefits are likely to be stable, they would have limited effect on the business cycle.

In the steady state, the inflationary effect of the Job Guarantee is not a concern under the fundamental argument that the government is bidding at a fixed price for wages. If wages in the private sector rise relative to the Job Guarantee wage, the relative wage differential rises, and so there will be tendency for workers to move to the private sector. This creates two mechanisms for inflation stabilisation: the workers add supply of labour in response to rising prices, and the total spending on Job Guarantee wages by the central government falls, reducing fiscal stimulus.

By offering a fixed price bid for labour, the possibility of wage deflation for lower-paid workers is almost certainly eliminated – rather than taking a pay cut, they will quit. (Highly compensated workers can have their pay cut, but this process will be short-circuited by the fact that their wages would eventually converge to the Job Guarantee wage.) Meanwhile, people moving to the Job Guarantee pool are raising government spending, and thus, automatically creating new fiscal stimulus.

Critics have noted that the Job Guarantee will stop damping inflation if the pool of workers (that are perceived as employable) drops to zero. Since this represents true full employment, that is hardly an outcome that I would spend a great deal of time worrying about. That said, the discussion is deferred to the chapter of MMT criticism, in Section 5.5.

... Initial Price Level Shock

The lack of worry about inflation in the steady state does not imply that there will be no price consequences of the Job Guarantee. The expectation is that there will be a one-time adjustment of wages for workers at the bottom end of the wage distribution.

Tcherneva (and her colleagues) currently suggest a $15/hour Job Guarantee wage in the United States – while the Federal minimum wage is $7.25/hour. (That Federal minimum wage is a bit of a dead letter; some states have much higher minimum wages already.) Given the likely possibility that many existing low-wage employers will have to pay a premium over the Job Guarantee wage (although that is hypothetical; we do not have empirical evidence of this effect), they will have no choice but to either raise wages and prices, suffer lower profit margins, or cease to exist.

Tcherneva argues in Chapter 5:

> *However, this one-time increase should not be confused with inflation – which is a continuous increase in the price level. Such a significant one-time wage increase would not be unprecedented. In 1949, the minimum wage was nearly doubled without accelerating inflation, at a time when the economy was as close to true full employment as it has ever been in the postwar era.*

It is highly predictable that employers that are directly affected by rising wages at the bottom of the income distribution will argue that this change would be cataclysmic. They will have to improve their utilisation of labour resources, which should be a positive for long-term productivity trends. Nevertheless, it appears implausible that the entire price structure would move in parallel with the rise of wages at the bottom. As such, linked price hikes (due to a rising wage bill) will be sector-specific, and not an across-the-board jump.

Real-World Programmes
Pavlina Tcherneva discusses similar programmes that were implemented in Chapter 5. She notes that most were temporary, other than India's National Rural Employment Guarantee Act (NREGA), although NREGA is not a universal programme.

Well-known temporary or small programmes included the New Deal (Depression era) and the Youth Incentive Entitlement Pilot Projects (1978-1980) in the United States, Argentina's Plan Jefes, Youth Job Guarantee in Brussels, zero long-term unemployment regions in France, and the first iteration of the 2009 Future Jobs Fund in the U.K. (it transitioned into "a punitive workfare programme"). Delving into the lessons that were learned in these programmes is beyond the scope of this text.

Standard Criticisms
The Case for a Job Guarantee notes a number of commonly raised criticisms. I will summarise some of them here.

- Tcherneva's response to the administrative difficulty is to observe that we do not believe that there is an optimal level of illiteracy; governments already undertake complex tasks to deal with pressing social issues.
- Some economists are worried about productivity. Tcherneva responds that leaving people unemployed is going to be less productive than giving people almost any somewhat useful job. A related question that I have come across (but not discussed in the book) is the argument that the number of workers in the Job Guarantee pool would be larger than (hypothetical) equilibrium unemployment. The argument was based upon neoclassical arguments about job searching. This is an interesting question, but it relies heavily upon the as-

sumption that neoclassical beliefs about the labour market are correct. Since MMT proponents dispute the notion of an "equilibrium" unemployment rate, resolving this debate would require a deep dive in the different approaches to labour market analysis, which is beyond the scope of this text.
- Another argument is that the jobs will be "make work" jobs. Tcherneva notes that there are two approaches: we can either look at whether the projects need to be completed, or we can approach the problem as being a guarantee for individuals. If we focus on projects, the calculus then naturally evolves towards hiring the best people for the job based on efficiency arguments. This mode of analysis makes sense for standard governmental programmes, but is not a good fit for the analysis of the Job Guarantee.
- Some people are concerned about robots taking all the jobs, and humans will not have any menial tasks left to do. (My opinion is that this is delusional propaganda pushed by the tech industry.)
- There are concerns that it would be difficult to respond to changing cyclical conditions. Firms already deal with the cycle (although they have the slightly simpler task of shutting down activities on short notice, rather than starting them up). Certain activities – like daycare – are not going to be possible with a rapidly rotating workforce. (Although one might imagine that under the assumption that the Job Guarantee offers childcare, some additional staff could be added. However, licensing/safety concerns would mean that people could not walk off the street straight into a childcare position.)
- Those on the left have several criticisms. One argument is that the Job Guarantee is yet another workfare scheme. Another argument relies upon the logic found in Michal Kalecki's essay "Political Aspects of Full Employment." In brief, Kalecki's argument is that capitalists would be deeply opposed to any policy that diminishes their power over workers. Pavlina Tcherneva observed that every increase in the rights of workers that we now take for granted (e.g., minimum wage, 5-day work week) were fought against by free market ideologues.

In my view, this is just an observation that is as unremarkable as saying that the sun rises in the east. Certain employers will be forced to radically change practices (or fail), but competitors who pay a good wage will benefit. Meanwhile, rising aggregate demand is good for business conditions. The coalition building is difficult, but in my opinion, not impossible.

The Job Guarantee Versus the Universal Basic Income
One policy that is often discussed in the context of the Job Guarantee is the possibility of paying a Universal Basic Income (UBI). Please note that this discussion represents my views and is not based on *The Case for a Job Guarantee*. Although I wanted to stick close to the source material, the UBI comes up so often in the context of the JG that I see a need to address the subject.

Although I would view the "consensus MMT position" as a preference for the Job Guarantee, opinions about the UBI vary. I am among those who are skeptical about the UBI. Note that I am discussing a UBI that lifts someone out of poverty without any other income sources; it is obvious that governments can make small transfers to all citizens without causing too much disruption (or do one-time cash transfers to counter recessions, which was the best possible response to the chaos of the 2020 pandemic lockdowns in many countries).

This is an old debate. For example, Hyman Minsky pointed out the difficulties with Milton Friedman's Negative Income Tax in the 1960s, while he preferred an Employer of Last Resort programme (which, to an outside observer, looks like a Job Guarantee). (Proponents of a UBI argue that the Negative Income Tax is different, but to an outside observer, the differences are cosmetic.)

A UBI has the advantage that it is simple – all citizens (of a certain age?) receive a monthly cheque from the central government (for the same amount). That is, there is no system of means testing (a current policy-making fad). In countries like Canada, senior citizens already receive such a benefit (in addition to the universal pension plan that pays based on contributions, as well as means-tested hardship benefits), a UBI just reduces the age at which the benefit is received.

My concern with the UBI is not "paying for it," but rather, basic multiplier analysis. A UBI has large implications for domestic demand. My argument is that the evidence is that a significant portion of the population has a high propensity to consume out of income, with most savings being generated by a smaller number of households (often with higher incomes). The implication is that there would be a much higher multiplier on UBI expenditures than is the case for policies like income tax cuts.

This aligns with Minsky's relatively traditional analysis that suggested that "... a negative income tax is expansionary or inflationary, even if budgets are balanced." That is, it is not enough to raise taxes to match the total spending on the UBI, the taxes raised would need to be larger than the expenditures (unless the government wanted to stimulate the economy, which might be a short-term objective). This would be particularly true if a wealth tax (for example) was used instead of raising income tax/value-added tax rates, since the brunt of the wealth tax would hit households with a low propensity to consume out of income.

If as I suspect, a broad-based income tax hike would be required to contain the inflationary pressures of the UBI, the result is that a significant portion of voters would face much higher marginal tax rates and end up with almost no net benefit. (That is, the UBI payments are largely matched by increased income taxes.). This is a very unattractive political mix, and it would be quite easy to agitate to lower the real value of the UBI in exchange for lower marginal tax rates. Since the premise of the UBI is that it would replace welfare state programmes, the ultimate result would just be the demise of social welfare programmes (explaining why libertarians love the proposal).

Concluding Remarks

Developed economies have been sluggish in recent decades, and persistent underemployment seems to be tied to this. A Job Guarantee would eliminate the problem of workers being forced into precarious jobs; firms need to provide legitimate work positions.

References and Further Reading

- *The Case for a Job Guarantee*, by Pavlina R. Tcherneva. Polity Press, 2020. ISBN: 13-978-1-5095-4211-6.
- "Political aspects of full employment," by Michal Kalecki. *New York and London* (1943).
- "The Macroeconomics of a Negative Income Tax." By Hyman P. Minsky (1969). Reprinted in *Ending Poverty: Jobs, Not Welfare*, 2013. Levy Economics Institute of Bard College. ISBN: 978-1-936192-30-4.

3.4 Green New Deal

The *Green New Deal* is a reform idea that has become associated with MMT, but one can be in favour of the Green New Deal and not MMT, and vice-versa. I am keeping this treatment brief, since most of the interesting parts of the discussion revolve around the programme's necessity – which is not a question of economic analysis.

Briefly, the Green New Deal is an attempt to ameliorate human-caused climatic change by restructuring the economy away from dependence on hydrocarbon energy. As such, it is a major technological challenge, as well as requiring some global cooperation. I lean towards pessimism about alternative energy, and the embarrassing response to the pandemic in 2020 has not raised my estimation about the odds of certain populations making sacrifices of any sort to respond to natural disasters.

Let's put aside the question of the necessity of reducing/eliminating carbon emissions, and just assume that society has set this as an objective, and assumes that incremental approaches (such as carbon taxes) are insufficient. The technological challenges associated with that objective are an engineering problem. It seems likely that most complaints about the Green New Deal would revolve around scientific questions, which is outside of the scope of this text.

Where MMT fits into the question is with respect to the economics of the plan: the mode of financing, how to marshal real resources, how to cushion the blow of the loss of industries that produce large amounts of greenhouse gas emissions.

Please note that this discussion is largely my commentary and is terse. I refer the reader to Tcherneva's *The Case for a Job Guarantee* for a summary that sticks closer to other MMT sources.

Economic Analysis

Since we are ruling out incremental approaches, a restructuring of the economy is required. There is no magic wand that will reduce the difficulties associated with this transition. Some activities that people like to undertake would have to be curtailed. However, this does not necessarily translate into the "economy doing badly" – at least how that phrase is normally interpreted – that is, the growth of Gross Domestic Product. GDP is the result of workers working and firms chasing after profits. Most advocates of free market economics emphasise the ability of capitalist economies to adapt to changing conditions. This argument seems plausible, and so it is reasonable to assume that nominal incomes will continue to grow.

There is a real question about standards of living. Modern industrial economies are built around exploiting the extremely high energy returns on investment (EROI) that hydrocarbons provide. (A high EROI implies that small energy inputs are required to generate large amounts of new energy.) If alternate energy sources have a lower EROI, we should expect to have less physical production. Since developed economies have shifted towards services, it is unclear how this affects the aggregates. However, measured economic data will have a hard time capturing such structural changes – the units of "real GDP" are not truly comparable between widely separated points in time. (This is known as the *index number problem*.) As such, the quantification of the effects on "standards of living" is fuzzy.

The analysis from an MMT perspective is based on what is happening with real resources. The restructuring consists of shutting down some industries, while growing others (mainly alternative energy sources and storage). Additionally, there is a need for environmental remediation, as well as an infrastructure build (e.g., flood protection).

The fact that there is a simultaneous opening and closing of industries helps make resource management slightly easier. Workers and investment will be shifted from declining industries towards new ones.

The implication is that the net draw on resources is less than what would be implied by estimating dollar costs for each change and adding them up. This addition of nominal dollars is easy, and it is a safe bet that is exactly how the programme would be treated in the business press. This is where the MMT-based analysis differs from conventional analysis – the real resource constraints matter, not dollar amounts.

The Job Guarantee would also provide a pool of labour and help reduce the blow of restructuring industries. However, a good portion of the infrastructure work would be done using capital-intensive processes, which is not a good fit for the Job Guarantee. However, Green New Deal proposals often have environmental remediation tasks that fit well with the Job Guarantee.

Implications

It would require a considerable amount of analysis to judge the implications of a Green New Deal proposal. Such work is beyond the scope of this text. An additional problem is that each proposal would need to be looked at separately, and the analysis would be specific to a country. I am not in a position to undertake such an analysis, and so I cannot offer an assessment of any such programme.

Realistically, any proposal would end up being some form of political compromise and might be less ambitious than plans floated by activists or think tanks. As such, there would be less than total mobilisation of national resources, and the analysis would be closer to that of other fiscal or infrastructure projects.

Any such plan would have the effect of increasing fixed investment by government, which would flip around the tendency for its shrinkage. There would be an added pressure on real resources, returning the economy closer to the "high pressure" state that was the feature of developed economies before the 1980s.

References and Further Reading
- Pavlina R. Tcherneva discusses the Green New Deal in *The Case for a Job Guarantee*, Polity Press, 2020. ISBN: 13-978-1-5095-4211-6.

3.5 Changing Governmental Financing Procedures

Proposals to abolish the (central) government bond market is one of the striking features of Modern Monetary Theory. One could argue that the immediate effects are limited in the current environment, given that rates are already near zero. I avoid attempting to be a forecaster, but it is safe to say that it would not be a true "surprise" if developed economy policy rates remained below 1% for a good portion of the 2020s. (This observation is consistent with bond market pricing at the time of writing.). This is a basic extrapolation of behaviour of past cycles. This cycle could be different, but it would not be a surprise if it is not. Meanwhile, some neoclassical economists are agitating for negative policy rates, which make the MMT proposal look much more sensible by contrast.

This ho-hum assessment does not align with popular discussion of MMT, with fears of "money printing" leading to hyperinflationary outcomes. For example, this is one of the suggested consequences within a resolution introduced by former U.S. senator David Perdue (URL: https://www.perdue.senate.gov/imo/media/doc/MMT%20Resolution.pdf).

As is typical of these discussions, the euro area is an exception to the discussion here. The euro floats versus other currencies, but the eurozone countries are pegged versus each other. The operations of the European central bank are enshrined in treaties, and the resulting dysfunction is a well-known problem. The problems with the structure of the euro – and how to improve the situation – is a complex story, and beyond the scope of this text. I would refer the reader to two books by MMT proponents (listed in the references at the end of this section) – Bill Mitchell and Dirk Ehnts – that offer an MMT analysis of the eurozone, and reform proposals. MMT proponents tend to be critical of the euro since it is a peg system.

Abolish (Central Government) Bonds!
My earlier book *Understanding Government Finance* covers the theoretical basis for the operations behind government bond issuance, and why it is possible to eliminate the issuance (Section 6.7). Most topics of interest were covered there, so I will keep the discussion here brief.

The starting point for MMT macroeconomics is to use the accounting procedure of consolidation – combining the balance sheets of the central bank and the fiscal arm of the government (the Treasury in the United States). Since the Treasury effectively owns the central bank in developed countries, this is entirely legitimate from an accounting perspective. Such ownership was typically not the case before World War II, and there are some privately-owned equity shares floating around for some central banks. (This does not include the U.S. Federal Reserve. Private banks are forced to buy preferred shares of the Federal reserve district banks as a form of capital requirement.) Nevertheless, some people object to consolidation (see Section 5.8), but it is justifiable assumption.

From this perspective, a government deficit implies that the government is emitting (central bank) settlement balances ("reserves" in American parlance) as the counterpart of the income flow imbalance. These settlement balances would pile up in the banking system (as is happening in the post-Quantitative Easing era). This has normally unwelcome side effects, so government bonds are issued to absorb the balances. This represents a transformation of governmental liabilities, from settlement balances to bonds/bills (the non-government balance sheet similarly shifts). By issuing bonds, the government creates a benchmark risk-free curve that is used in pricing private sector interest rates. This also allows the central bank the ability to attempt to steer the economy with interest rate policy (as noted in Section 2.5, MMT proponents are largely unconvinced by the effectiveness of interest rate policy).

This background leads to the proposal: stop issuing bonds, and let the risk-free curve disappear (other than settlement balances, which pay 0%).

Implementation Details

For good reasons, civil servants and elected politicians must follow procedural rules with regard to spending money. As such, there is a web of laws and regulations that constrain governmental financial transactions. Under those regulations, the central bank and fiscal arm of government are distinct, and financial flows must follow certain forms.

This is normally the key argument of critics: we cannot consolidate the fiscal arm of government and the central bank because of the operations of those rules. This shows a complete lack of imagination: regulations were made by legislative bodies, and they can be changed in the same fashion.

The simplest work around is for the fiscal arm of government to be given an open-ended overdraft at the central bank. At one stroke, the problem disappears. Meanwhile, this is not novel: such overdraft facilities were common before superstitious beliefs about government finance led to their abolishment.

Consequences

I see two main consequences of such reforms.

1. Since the fiscal arm of government has no debt instruments outstanding, default is no longer even a hypothetical possibility. Since there was no practical way of such a government to be forced into involuntary default, the practical effect of this is not large. However, it eliminates the possibility of using government debt worries as a political tactic.
2. Interest rate policy no longer exists, and so cannot be used to control inflation. This is a source of obvious distress to conventional economists, while most MMT proponents view this to be a small loss. One way to avoid this outcome is for the central bank to issue its own bonds, and/or pay interest on settlement balances. This still leaves the fiscal agency immune to default, while interest rate policy might continue. However, it still leaves central bankers the ability to hijack fiscal policy dis-

cussions by making arbitrary threats about raising interest rates.

Given that I am not expecting rapid rises in interest rates in the absence of much looser fiscal policy, these changes might be viewed as cosmetic over the medium-term. That assessment would not be shared by conventional economists. Much of the arguments about the effects of such a policy rely on beliefs about inflation and the behaviour of politicians, which is discussed in Chapter 5.

One Trillion Dollars!

One eye-catching financial reform for the U.S. Federal Government that was originally floated online by Carlos Mucha during one of the periodic debt ceiling crises is the notion of minting a trillion-dollar coin. During the pandemic crisis of 2020, Congresswoman Rashida Tlaib introduced a motion to mint two trillion-dollar coins.

The trillion-dollar coin comes out of the legal details of monetary institutional arrangements in the United States. The U.S. Treasury (the fiscal arm of the government) issues coins. For other metals, coin denominations are fixed by law. However, the Treasury has the right to issue platinum coin in any denomination. (These are already issued for collectors.)

The Treasury pockets the profits on the difference between the face value of the coin and the cost to produce it. This is the literal version of seigneurage (also spelled seigniorage) profits. (Economists also refer to the carry profits by the central bank as seigneurage, but that is a different concept. The profits made from minting coins is the traditional version of seigneurage.)

All the Treasury needs to do is take a small amount of platinum (with maybe $200 worth of the metal), that it then mints into a coin with a $1-trillion face value. It then ships it to the Federal Reserve (like it does other coins) – under close guard – and the Treasury just cleared a profit of close to $1 trillion. (The existence of such coins could give rise to future action movie plots.)

This eliminates two institutional barriers to Treasury spending – the need to replenish the Treasury's balance at the Fed, and the debt limit (since coins do not count).

This procedure is economically equivalent to the Fed giving a $1-trillion overdraft in exchange for a small disc of platinum with somebody's mug stamped on it. The important thing to note is that this possibility demonstrates how arbitrary the rules governing intra-governmental accounting are. (As Rohan Grey observed in response to an online draft of this text, the coin has some advantages over an overdraft. However, these refer to political/legal issues in the United States, while the economic outcome appears to be the same.)

If we look at other countries, the rules are different, and so the means to bypass them correspondingly change.

Concluding Remarks

For online discussions, "money printing" is synonymous with MMT. The reality is that very few people who invoke "money printing" have any idea of the legal or operational framework behind government borrowing, so such discussions are often a waste of time. The issue of losing interest rate policy exists, but that would be a more complex debate. Once again, I refer the reader to Chapter 5 for coverage of these debates.

References and Further Reading
- My book *Understanding Government Finance* covers this area in depth.
- For an example of press coverage of Representative Tlaib's proposal, see https://fortune.com/2020/03/25/coronavirus-stimulus-bill-how-will-us-pay-trillion-dollar-coin/
- The following working paper by L. Randall Wray notes how an overdraft at the central bank is equivalent to other schemes. Wray, L. Randall. "Central bank independence: Myth and misunderstanding." Levy Economics Institute, Working Paper 791 (2014). URL: http://www.levyinstitute.org/pubs/wp_791.pdf
- Chapter 4 of *Modern Monetary Theory: A Primer on Macroeconomics for Sovereign Monetary Systems* by L. Randall Wray covers fiscal operations. Palgrave-Macmillan, 2012. ISBN: 978-1-137-26514-2.
- *Eurozone dystopia: groupthink and denial on a grand scale*, by William Mitchell. Edward Elgar Publishing, 2015. ISBN: 978-1-78471-666-0
- *Modern Monetary Theory and European Macroeconomics,* by Dirk H. Ehnts, *Routledge,* 2017. ISBN: 978-1-315-62303-0

3.6 Guessing About the Future

I avoid pretending to be a forecaster, and so I do not claim to know what will happen in the coming years. Nevertheless, we can frame our thinking in a systematic fashion.

The baseline is the continuation of previous trends: fiscal policy tapering off, coupled with the consensus chewing over every possible variant of monetary policy. The economy would likely expand, but job growth would be tepid, and wage growth quite low.

One could imagine the private sector finding some activity that requires heavy investment, which puts the economy closer to a high-pressure state. Roughly speaking, a return to the late-1990s situation, where there was a broad-based expansion in investment (although "tech" got most of the headlines). This is the dream scenario for investment bank economists, and so it will always be close to a consensus medium-term outlook.

There are many possible disaster scenarios (too depressing to list the many possibilities) that could lead to slow growth or recession. Sooner or later, there will be another recession, but it is too early to sketch out the scenarios.

The main remaining plausible scenario involves a renewed emphasis on fiscal policy to put at least some developed countries onto a faster growth path. The rise of MMT suggests there is a growing constituency for such an approach, and arguably some segments of the mainstream are moving in that direction. The relative ease of ramping up government spending in response to the 2020 pandemic will obviously make arguments about "how will we pay for this?" look weak.

The interesting question about this scenario is whether spending will be blunt "aggregate demand management" – mainly helping sectors and regions that are already growing – or the MMT approach, aimed at reducing widespread underemployment.

Weighing the odds of scenarios is the main analytical problem.

- Disaster scenarios largely appear to be hard-to-forecast tail events, although some might be predictable by methods outside of economics (e.g., climate science).
- Judging the probability of a private sector investment boom is generally the focus of equity strategists, and I long ago gave up on trying to understand equities. The problem for the private sector boom story is that if it is going to tighten the labour market, the developments need to create jobs. However, most of the excitement in equities revolves around replacing labour. My argument is that you need a new product that implies a labour-intensive rollout. Since new prod-

ucts pop up all the time, this is not completely far-fetched.
- The remaining plausible scenario is the possibility of expansive fiscal policies. During most of the time of preparation of this manuscript, fiscal policy settings were loose (certainly compared to previous decades), and the complaints about this were largely muffled. The possibility of mass default outcome was entirely likely, and such an event would be dangerous for the banks that employ bank economists. Going forward, the willingness to expand fiscal policy is likely to depend upon the country. It is possible that there could be a wave of similar policies – as happened in the past – but if policy changes are incremental, the direction of policy may diverge more. When I was finishing the manuscript, President Biden announced a large fiscal relief programme, with some long-lasting reforms such as a rise in the national minimum wage. I cannot predict how much of this will end up implemented, but the signal is that there is a step towards the policies discussed in this chapter.

My bias has always been to expect institutional inertia. However, American politics is currently in flux (I am writing this just after the inauguration of President Biden). We are suddenly seeing movements away from the consensus fiscal conservatism position. That said, it is unclear to me whether these sentiments will survive the likely bounce in growth that should happen as a significant portion of the population has been vaccinated.

Chapter 4 What Is MMT? (Longer Version)

4.1 Introduction

This chapter offers a longer description of Modern Monetary Theory than what was provided in Section 1.2. This description is not meant to be comprehensive, and some content appears in other chapters. The decision was made to defer this content to a later chapter because I wanted to focus on real-world policy concerns first, to demonstrate why the theory matters. Otherwise, it is easy to get derailed in wrangling about abstract theoretical points.

In Section 1.2, I drew the distinction between "narrow MMT" and "broad MMT." My interests (and most internet debates) revolve around "narrow MMT," and so the bulk of the material is tied to that area. However, Section 4.6 outlines some other areas of interest.

The following major topics are of interest but are discussed in other chapters. Correspondingly, this chapter is deceptively short.

- The Job Guarantee is the key distinguishing concept that helps define MMT relative to broad post-Keynesian thinking. Section 3.3 describes the Job Guarantee, but the discussion in this chapter explains the theoretical significance attached to the concept by MMT proponents.
- Functional Finance was summarised in Section 1.2. More details can be found in *Understanding Government Finance*, and concerns about it are discussed in Chapter 5.
- The MMT literature discusses the operational details of government financing (as well as the operation of the banking system). Section 3.5 discusses the key insight: that floating currency sovereigns only face self-imposed limitations on their finance. There are many primers available that run through the accounting of operations (including *Understanding Government Finance*).
- MMT proponents correctly observe that government liabilities are an asset of the "non-central government sector." These are often referred to as "net financial assets." Furthermore, sectoral ac-

counting identities are linked to this. There is a surprising amount of controversy surrounding this (since accounting identities are true by definition), and I defer this discussion to Section 5.9.
- Developmental economics and open economy concerns are discussed in Section 5.10.
- Finally, a scattering of other topics also appears in Chapter 5.

4.2 The Mosler *White Paper*

Warren Mosler, one of the founders of Modern Monetary Theory (MMT) has published a white paper that acts as a summary of narrow MMT. It is available at: http://mosleconomics.com/mmt-white-paper/ It is brief (1300 words) and meets the objective of offering an overview of the question "What is MMT?" for more advanced readers. Its contents can be used to define narrow MMT, but as I discuss in Section 4.6, this is missing a lot of supporting material. One could view the *White Paper* as being a set of minimal principles that constitute MMT, which can then be supplemented with other theory.

Another point to note about the *White Paper* is that it is terse (certainly unlike my preferred writing style). Since I am familiar with the arguments, I can easily follow the logic, but others might be tripped up.

Summary

Mosler answers the question "What is MMT?" as follows.

> *MMT began largely [as] a description of monetary operations, which are best thought of as debits and credits to accounts kept by banks, businesses, and individuals.*
>
> *Warren Mosler independently originated what has been popularized as MMT in 1992. And while subsequent research has revealed writings of authors who had similar thoughts on some of MMT's understanding and insights, including Abba Lerner, George Knapp, Mitchell Innes, Adam Smith, and former NY Fed chief Beardsley Ruml, MMT is unique in its analysis of monetary economies, and therefore best considered as its own school of thought.*

To give further background: Warren Mosler is a successful fixed income investor who developed the ideas around MMT independently of the other founders, William Mitchell and Randall Wray, who were academics, within the broad post-Keynesian school of thought.

According to the *White Paper*, the key difference between MMT and other schools of thought relies upon the following observations. This might be referred to as the "operational core" of MMT.

> *MMT alone recognizes that the US Government and its agents are the only supplier of that which it demands for payment of taxes.*
>
> *That is, the currency itself is a simple public monopoly.*
>
> *The US government levies taxes payable in US dollars.*
>
> *The US dollars to pay those taxes or purchase US Treasury securities can only originate from the US government and its agents.*
>
> *The economy has to sell goods, services or assets to the US government (or borrow from the US government) or it will not be able to pay its taxes or purchase US Treasury securities.*

The *White Paper* (at least the version I used) specifically states "the U.S."; this should really refer to a "currency sovereign." Currency sovereignty needs to be thought of as a spectrum, and the freedom of action of most governments faces some constraints. That said, it is safe to say that countries with a currency peg or that borrow in a foreign currency have no currency sovereignty. Euro countries have created an internal peg system that eliminates currency sovereignty of the members (although the larger countries have some capacity to ignore the constraints of the system). When we look at most non-euro developed countries, they have extensive currency sovereignty.

The operational core captures a great deal of what is argued about in popular MMT debates. However, the discussion of the price level is an important component of narrow MMT.

> *Only MMT recognizes the source of the price level. The currency itself is a public monopoly. Monopolists are necessarily "price setters."*
>
> Therefore: **The price level is necessarily a function of prices paid by the government's agents when it spends, or collateral demanded when it lends.** [emphasis in original]
>
> *In a market economy the government need only set one price, letting market forces continuously determine all other prices as expressions of relative value, as further influenced by institutional structure.*

If one wants to discuss "what is new in MMT?" this is where one really needs to start. I discuss the theory of price level determination in the next section. However, critiques of MMT typically stay focussed on the operational aspects.

Monetary Operations: Implications and Debate

The key implication of monetary operations analysis is that currency sovereigns cannot be forced to involuntarily default for financial reasons. Instead, the constraint on fiscal policy is the inflationary consequences – which will include the cost of imported goods.

The *White Paper* lists implications of operations analysis as follows.

> *1. The US government and its agents, from inception, necessarily spend (or lend) first, only then can taxes be paid or US Treasury securities purchased.*
>
> *This is in direct contrast to the rhetoric that states the US government must tax to get US dollars to spend, and what it doesn't tax it must borrow from the likes of China and leave the debt to our grandchildren.*
>
> *MMT therefore recognizes that it's not the US government that needs to get dollars to spend, but instead, the driving force is that taxpayers need the US government's dollars to be able to pay taxes and purchase US Treasury securities.*
>
> *2. Crowding out private spending or private borrowing, driving up interest rates, federal funding requirements and solvency issues are not applicable for a government that spends first, and then borrows.*

One way to summarise the implications of operations analysis is that default risk is not meaningful, regardless of the level of the debt-to-GDP ratio. If we look at conventional analyses of fiscal policy (at least historically), we see the opposite – there is considerable alarm about the level of the debt-to-GDP ratio, and the objective of fiscal policy is to steer that ratio.

Role of Interest Rates

From a fixed income practitioner's perspective, the most eye-catching part of Mosler's work is the discussion of interest rates.

> *MMT recognizes that a positive policy rate results in a payment of interest that can be understood as "basic income for those who already have money."*
>
> *MMT recognizes that with government a net payer of interest, higher interest rates can impart an expansionary, inflationary (and regressive) bias through two types of channels -- interest income channels and forward pricing channels. This means that what's called "Fed tightening" by increasing rates may increase total spending and foster price increases, contrary to the advertised intended effects of reducing demand and bringing down inflation. Likewise, lowering rates removes interest income from the economy which works to reduce demand and bring down inflation, again contrary to advertised intended effects.*
>
> *MMT understands that a permanent 0% policy rate is the base case for analysis for a floating exchange rate policy.*

Note that Mosler suggests that interest rates *may* work in the opposite way assumed by conventional analysis, as noted in Section 2.5. The role of interest rates in steering the economy is a topic that should be of far more interest. Why did the economy not accelerate, even though there was a multi-year period of negative real interest rates?

The analysis of a permanent 0% interest rate policy (PZIRP) is another topic that does not receive enough attention. For example, critics will discuss an out-of-control spiral due to surging interest rates. If the nominal interest rate on government liabilities is locked at 0%, how does such a spiral happen?

Concluding Remarks

The Mosler *White Paper* on MMT offers a summary of what I refer to as narrow MMT. The narrowness of definition has the advantage of focusing on core concepts that are accepted by almost all MMT proponents (although whether there are literary objections to the wording is uncertain). For some people, it is an advantage that the *White Paper* has some wiggle room that would allow it to be re-interpreted using mathematical tools that are part of neoclassical economics. Nevertheless, when someone like me refers to "MMT," we are typically referring to the broader tradition, which is more post-Keynesian in spirit. That post-Keynesian tradition rejects the mathematical modelling assumptions used by neoclassicals, making *rapprochement* much more difficult.

References and Further Reading
- *White Paper: Modern Monetary Theory (MMT)*. Warren Mosler. I worked with a copy dated 2019-11-11. URL: http://moslereconomics.com/mmt-white-paper/

4.3 Price Level Determination

The determination of the price level is an important claim within Warren Mosler's *MMT White Paper* (previous section). From a theoretical perspective, the theory of price level determination is a key feature that distinguishes MMT from other approaches to economic theory. This theory is related to the Job Guarantee framework (Section 3.3). The argument is that one could come up with the suggestion for a Job Guarantee policy from any number of directions, the emphasis within MMT is the link to stabilising inflation.

Verbally, the concept is that the government fixes a *key* price, which it can do courtesy of its monopoly on (base) money creation. Other prices within the economy are set relative to this price. This section will outline a simplified Monetary Monopoly Model, which is based on descriptions elsewhere, as well as the article "Monopoly Money: The State as a Price Setter" by Pavlina R. Tcherneva. I have simplified the discussion to allow the elimination of the use of equations. It would be a straightforward exercise to attach equations to what I describe herein.

The model I outline is not meant to be one that could fit real-world data. Rather, it is the simplest possible canonical model that captures the price-setting mechanism. If one wanted to create a more realistic model, the next step would be a model of the Job Guarantee. Given that we have not had a full implementation of a Job Guarantee in a developed country, the mathematical structure of such a model is obviously open to debate, with no easy way to resolve disputes.

Backstory: Introduction of a New Currency

To visualise what is happening in this simple model, imagine that a country wants to introduce a brand-new currency, conveniently labelled the "dollar." No (local currency) dollars were previously in existence, although we assume that there is a private sector that already engaged in commerce. For example, the commerce may have been a gift exchange economy, or perhaps the locals used the Polish zloty.

Why would a country do such a thing? One example is how colonial powers introduced currencies to requisition local labour and goods as well as to force the population into Western norms of behaviour. The Tcherneva article and the book *Understanding Modern Money* by L. Randall Wray discuss this brutal history. The use of money as a means of intermediation as part of the requisitioning process has organisational advantages over direct requisition (e.g., the difference between drafting soldiers versus paying volunteers).

Model Assumptions

The model assumptions are limited.
- The model is of the "dollar economy," and the government has a monopoly on the creation of these dollars, and the initial stock of dollars in the hands of the "private sector" is zero.
- The government imposes a fixed lump sum tax on the populace, and the threat of sanctions means that the tax will be paid. For simplicity,

we assume that there is no counterfeiting, tax evasion, fraud, or bankruptcies. (This is standard for a mathematical economic model, but in a verbal model, this clause eliminates many "what if?" objections.)
- The government wants labourers to show up at a workplace, and it pays a fixed $1 per hour. (This price was an arbitrary decision by the government – there are no pre-existing dollar prices to compare this to.)
- The government does not lend to the private sector.
- The time period of the model is weekly, and the aggregate lump sum tax to be paid is $1000 by the end of the week.
- The model does not consider other transactions in the economy.

The First Week

Since we assume that the $1000 lump sum tax is paid, and that the initial stock of dollars outside the government sector is zero, the populace *must* provide *at least* 1000 hours of labour. Otherwise, the populace in aggregate is short dollars, and since it cannot borrow dollars from the government, and we assume no defaults that labour income must be earned.
- The simplest case is that exactly 1000 hours are worked, and so the private sector ends up with a balance of $0. The next week starts with exactly the same state as the first week, and the previous logic repeats.
- Alternatively, the populace would provide more than 1000 hours of labour. The excess ends up saved in the form of government-issued dollars. This pre-existing stock of assets needs to be accounted for in the next week. The logic for this case is discussed later.

The previous statements all *had* to be true, under the previous assumptions. However, we cannot be sure about the exact mechanism by which the private sector provides those labour hours. Two example possibilities are as follows.
- Each household sends representatives to work to meet its own share of the lump sum tax and turns over labour earnings immediately to meet the tax obligation.
- Labourers show up to earn dollars in excess of their own share of the tax bill, and they exchange the excess to others in some fashion. For example, if there was a pre-existing zloty economy,

they would trade dollars for zloty, and thus the dollars are an exchanged asset within the *unmodelled* zloty economy. The zloty wage rates versus the government-paid dollar wage rate would be an obvious fundamental relative price driving the exchange rate.

Having the private sector immediately surrender all their dollars each week partly defeats the purpose of introducing a currency. The hope is that more hours would be worked, to create a stock of dollars that would then be exchanged within the private sector.

In any event, the government has accomplished its goal. It has gotten (at least) 1000 hours of labour effort, solely based on the enforcement of tax laws, while not having to offer anything of real value in exchange.

Second Week: Excess Money Case

The reasonable expectation is that more hours would be worked in the initial weeks, to create a surplus of dollars in the private sector that could be used to meet future shortfalls. For example, 1500 hours could be worked, to generate an excess of $500 at the end of the week. In that case, the logic is different. The government can only be guaranteed that 500 hours of labour will be provided – since the private sector can run down its existing balance. However, it is guaranteed that there will have been a cumulative 2000 hours worked by the end of the second week, with the excess of 2000 hours equalling the stock of dollars held by the private sector at the end of week two.

For the model to predict the number of hours worked, we need to add behavioural assumptions: how large a stock of dollars does the private sector want to hold at the end of the week? Since there is an infinite number of behavioural functions, this branches into an infinite number of models. For a simple example, Sam Levey has developed one example (URL: https://medium.com/@slevey087/monopoly-money-redux-a4d96f156f7).

Since the described situation is far removed from the situation in most real-world economies, there is no need to pursue the details of a behavioural function. Rather, the key characteristic of the model is that the government applies a carrot-and-stick approach to money: it creates money (the carrot) to requisition desired goods/services/labour at a fixed price, and it uses taxes (the stick) to drive the demand for money.

Banks Do Not Affect the Story (Much)

As a lead-in to the discussion in Section 5.7(of whether MMT ignores banking, the existence of a banking system will not affect the number of hours that have to be provided, even though "banks create money." The reason why is straightforward: even if banks layered dollar-denominated deposits on top of government money, the payment of tax bills requires the banks to send *government* money to the government on behalf of depositors. (If a central bank existed, this would be a transfer of settlement balances at the central bank.) There is no way for the bank to get that government money without somebody first providing the labour hours, that later makes its way to the bank. Remember that we assume that there are no defaults, and the government does not lend dollars to the private sector.

One may note that in the real world, central banks do lend dollars to banks, as shows up in the Mosler *White Paper*: "The US government and its agents, from inception, necessarily spend (or lend) first...." Central banks lend against collateral, and so the collateral policy would need to be considered in price level determination if we added it to the model. (The lending policy would need to respect the price rule, and so this implies needing to add behavioural relationships between interest rates and prices, etc.) This would greatly complicate the behavioural relationships.

To Be Interesting, the Price Set Must Be Significant

We do not normally need a model of how a government can provision itself using a tax and a fixed price. We want to have a model of the whole economy. To be interesting, we need to add other goods and services, as well as wage rates, to the mix. This can be done in any number of ways – and greatly increases the complexity of the model.

For the fixed price core of the model to be interesting, it needs to be a significant part of the aggregate economy. If it is, then we should see some form of model relationship between the fixed price and the other prices within the economy.

This is where the Job Guarantee comes in. The Job Guarantee wage is meant to be a living wage, and so it is directly competitive with all low wage jobs. As a result, the government has the hope of directly influencing the wage structure of the economy – which then feeds through to the prices of final output.

As such, the simplified Monetary Monopoly Model points in the direction of any number of possible Job Guarantee models. However, the key dynamic that should be common to all of these models is that a *key price* is being set as a policy variable.

Government as a Price Taker?

The obvious concern with applying the Monetary Monopoly Model to the real world is the following: what happens if the government is a price taker? That is, it lets the price of everything it requisitions to be set "in the market?"

From a theoretical perspective, if we look at the simplest models where the government is a price taker, the price level ends up being indeterminate. That is, any number could be used to satisfy the model equations. For example, the Real Business Cycle (RBC) model found in Chapter 2 of Jordi Galí's *Monetary Policy, Inflation, and the Business Cycle*. (The indeterminacy of the price level in RBC models is more worrisome to outsiders like Warren Mosler and myself than it is to neoclassicals.) This indeterminacy explains Warren Mosler's comments in his *White Paper* about recognising the source of the price level. Neoclassicals have various methods to get around this indeterminacy, but they are largely mathematical kludges.

Although price level indeterminacy is not seen in the real world, one could argue that if the government runs its requisitioning strategy in a fashion that completely ignores its effect on the price structure, one might expect rapid inflation (e.g., unstable prices). This would be one high-level interpretation of the inflationary experience of the 1960s-1970s – albeit highly simplified.

Meanwhile, the reality is that most government spending does feature a fixed price element. Prices paid are fixed, although perhaps for a shorter period. An ambitious modeller might attempt to show how having the government chase prices in the private sector – e.g., price taking behaviour – destabilises the model economy. In other words, *doing exactly what conventional economists tell governments to do* helps generate inflationary pressures in the economy.

Concluding Remarks

The Monetary Monopoly Model is the simplest model that captures key distinctive elements of MMT thinking. If one insists on using mathematical approaches, the differences between price-taking policies and price-setting policies needs to be examined.

Technical Digressions

- I included the possibility of a pre-existing currency to make the backstory more plausible. Even in the historical colonial situation, state money is pushing out existing economic practices. Monopolies are not complete – things like Bitcoin exist – but competitor currencies in legal developed economies are generally insignificant. The other reason to add in the digression is to point out the "exchange rate" problem between the government-set price and prices in the private sector. For example, for a Job Guarantee model to be interesting, we need a private sector wage and the Job Guarantee wage. Since working in the private sector or working in the Job Guarantee are competing real economy transactions, there should be behavioural constraints on the relative wage rates.
- The model features lump sum taxes, which I normally reject as unrealistic. Simplicity is one excuse, and the other is that if we imposed a more realistic tax (e.g., an income tax), we would need to have a better handle on the private sector economy, as well as some idea about the behaviour of the private sector within the model. To have an estimate of the amount of goods/labour it can requisition, the government needs at least a rough idea how large the tax take will be. If we are discussing real-world economies, we normally will have an idea of what taxes will be paid, unless they are completely novel (e.g., taxes on cannabis sales after they were legalised in Canada) or contingent on hard-to-predict events (e.g., capital gains taxes).
- Price level indeterminacy arises in RBC models because the behavioural equations (derived on optimising behaviour assumptions) all imply constraints on relative prices: between the generic good prices and wages, and between spot and future goods prices. (There is also a relative balance sheet constraint between money and bond holdings.) However, the initial price level could be set to any level, and every other price just adjusts proportionally. One can point to three ways to eliminate this issue. The first method is the controversial Fiscal Theory of the Price Level, which creates other problems for the plausibility of the model. (The Fiscal Theory of the Price Level implies that the price level should immediately jump every time fiscal policy settings are tweaked, which obviously does

not happen. Feeble attempts to explain away this discrepancy are incorrect.) The second is to impose a money demand component to the objective function that creates a demand for money, and since the initial stock of inherited money is fixed, forces the initial price to a particular value. The problem with this is that households essentially get a fixed amount of utility of holding a $10 bill, which does not match the reality that a fiat currency could be re-denominated and nothing much would happen. The third obvious possibility is to invoke price stickiness – e.g., the Calvo price-setting mechanism. However, every treatment of the Calvo mechanism I have seen was purely forward-looking – there were not inherited fixed prices that would provide an initial scaling. The possibility of inherited fixed prices creates difficulties with finding a solution. There are more advanced ways of attacking this problem, but they are either somewhat unsatisfactory (argle-bargle about equilibria) or moving the model away from the canonical model roots.

References and Further Reading:
- *White Paper: Modern Monetary Theory (MMT)*. Warren Mosler. I worked with a copy dated 2019-11-11. URL: http://mosleronomics.com/mmt-white-paper/
- "Monopoly Money: The State as a Price Setter," by Pavlina R. Tcherneva. Oeconomicus, Volume V, Winter 2002
- *Understanding Modern Money: The Key to Full Employment and Price Stability* by L. Randall Wray. Edward Elgar, 1998. ISBN: 978-1-84542-941-6
- "Monopoly Money Redux," by Sam Levey, July 17, 2020. URL: https://medium.com/@slevey087/monopoly-money-redux-a4d96f156f7
- *Monetary Policy, Inflation, and the Business Cycle: An Introduction to the New Keynesian Framework*, by Jordi Galí. Princeton University Press, 2008. ISBN: 978-0-691-13316-4.

4.4 Fiscal Sustainability

One frequently encounters variations of the phrase "unsustainable debt trajectory" (or similar) in statements by mainstream economists. The phrase is popular as it offers what appears to be a sophisticated criticism of a fiscal policy stance that is disapproved of, but without having any substantive content that can be used to rebut the speaker. Modern Monetary Theory (MMT) largely rejects that "debt sustainability" has theoretical validity for a floating currency sovereign.

This section leans mainly on a paper by Scott Fullwiler to describe the MMT stance (along with a pre-print that was released at the time of writing). However, the wording is largely my own, and I have greatly simplified the discussion to be an outline of the MMT stance. I have simplified the arguments for a straightforward reason: unlike the academic articles by Fullwiler, I make no assumption that the reader is familiar with the mainstream views that Fullwiler is debating. I want to avoid delving too deep into the mainstream theory around sustainability, since I find it to be extremely weak.

Debt Sustainability

The concept of "debt sustainability" is the usual alternative to the argument that inflation is the only constraint on floating currency sovereigns. This section is based on some of the discussions found in the paper "The debt ratio and sustainable macroeconomic policy," by Scott Fullwiler, albeit with simplifications.

One of the issues with "fiscal sustainability" is that there is not a single agreed-upon formal definition. If we do not know what "fiscal sustainability" means, we have a hard time discussing the topic. One formal version of "debt sustainability" is the so-called inter-temporal governmental budget constraint (IGBC) of neoclassical literature. It should be noted that the IGBC is controversial, even within the neoclassical literature. If one wanted to have a sophisticated discussion of economic theory, it would be in respect to the IGBC. However, this is being skipped in this text, for the following reasons.

- If the reader is familiar with the IGBC, the Fullwiler paper discusses its shortcomings. (Section 7.4 of my book *Understanding Government Finance* also discusses the IGBC.) My feeling is that if the reader is familiar with the IGBC, they are also likely to be familiar with the critiques.
- If the reader is unfamiliar with the IGBC, it can be summarised as: incorrect and/or misleading, smothered in obscure mathematics. I see no need to confuse readers with defunct concepts.

As a result, this section will only discuss a simpler-to-understand version of "sustainability." This definition of fiscal sustainability is that the interest expenditures implied by government debt are not supposed to rise beyond the productive capacity of the economy, or alternatively, the debt-to-GDP ratio does not become arbitrarily large (the ratio "goes to infinity"). Since the interest expenditures/debt-to-GDP ratio are essentially equivalent, I will focus on the version that uses the debt-to-GDP ratio.

(A point about terminology. Interest spending by governments is typically called the "interest burden" by mainstream economists, which is a good example of how mainstream economists insert moral judgements within their "scientific" terminology.)

The first thing to keep in mind is that we are discussing the ratio of debt-to-GDP, and if we assume that the economy is growing forever, both the level of debt and the size of nominal GDP will become arbitrarily large ("go to infinity"). As such, we should not care about the absolute level of debt (but that does not stop fiscal conservatives).

In less formal discussions, mainstream commentators are typically using a looser version of this definition. The issue is not what is happening at times infinitely far in the future, rather a concern about the debt-ratio on some forecast horizon (like 75 years). Shortening the horizon is reasonable, as we should not be worried about what is happening to government debt long after the Sun has reduced the Earth to a cinder. However, by moving away from this formal definition, "fiscal sustainability" is quite vague, and it does not have much more theoretical content. It is equivalent to exclaiming, "Good golly, the debt-to-GDP ratio will be really high!" (What ratios qualify as "really high"? Why do we care?)

Primary Deficits and Long-Run Averages

We cannot really hope to create an exact forecast of the long-run trajectory of the economy. We might be able to get a handle on the upcoming year or so, but after that, forecasts get fuzzier. The usual convention is to assume that the economy will revert to a long-run average behaviour. This is defensible, although one could question the standard way this is done.

- We assume that the economy follows an average nominal or real growth rate. Economists tend to love working with real quantities, so the typical variable is the real growth rate, normally denoted g.
- The next assumption is that interest rates also have a long-term average. If we look at real GDP, we need to look at real interest rates, with the long-term average typically denoted r.

- Government non-interest spending is assumed to be a steady percentage of GDP.
- The tax take is also assumed to be a fixed percentage of GDP. An astute reader will note: should not the tax rate be set at a level consistent with a desired average inflation rate? This is of course the correct answer – but we need to do things incorrectly to understand conventional fiscal analysis.

There are two key implications of the above assumptions. The first is that the difference between the interest rate and the growth rate (typically denoted $r - g$) is critically important for analysis (as will be seen). The second implication is that there is an expectation that the primary fiscal balance – taxes minus non-interest expenses – is a constant percentage of GDP. (The fiscal balance is the primary balance with interest expense subtracted.) Academics will often jump right into discussing this topic in terms of the primary fiscal balance and the importance of *r-g* without explaining why they are looking at those quantities.

Debt-Ratio Dynamics

The question then turns to: how does the debt-to-GDP ratio evolve under those steady-state conditions? The actual equations are relatively simple, but messy. It is easier to discuss an approximation of the dynamics. The assumption is that we want to calculate the debt-to-GDP ratio on an annual basis.

As a simplification, I listened to my advice to abolish money from economic theory, and I assume that there is no money issuance. One could incorporate money (a liability with an interest rate of 0%) in two easy ways: either by assuming that the money/debt ratio is constant (which implies that we just use the weighted average interest rate of all liabilities as r), or assume that money creation is a constant percentage of GDP – which cancels out an equivalent amount of the primary balance. More complex solutions require incorporation of some kind of dynamics that moves us away from a steady state condition.

The next year's debt-to-GDP ratio (or liability-to-GDP ratio) is (roughly) given by the following two steps.
1. Take the ratio as a number (e.g., a 50% ratio is 0.5), and compound this number by the (*r-g*) differential. If the differential is 2%, then the ratio goes from 0.5 to 0.5(1.02) = 0.51 (or 51%).

In other words, this term has the ratio growing at the interest rate/growth rate spread.
2. Subtract the primary fiscal balance (or add the primary fiscal deficit) as a percentage of GDP to the above figure (as a percentage). If we continue the previous example, and the assumed primary surplus is 2% of GDP, we then subtract 2% from 51% to get a new debt-to-GDP ratio of 49%.

With low interest/growth rates, the above procedure gives numbers that are close enough for government work. As a reminder: if one insists on adding money creation, one needs to pick the rule that determines the growth of the money stock. If the money/debt ratio is constant, just replace government debt-to-GDP ratio with the government liability-to-GDP ratio, and use the weighted average interest rate in the Step 1 calculation. Otherwise, if money growth is a fixed percentage of GDP, subtract (money growth plus the primary balance) in Step 2.

We can now ask: under what conditions can the debt-to-GDP ratio go to infinity?

- If $r<g$, the ratio cannot go to infinity – *no matter how large the primary fiscal deficit is*. The reason is that the compounding step (Step 1 in the calculation) will eventually imply such a large drop in the ratio, that the primary deficit cannot push it above the previous level. For example, if $r-g$ is -1%, and the primary deficit is 10% of GDP, if the debt-GDP ratio started at 2000%, it would be (2000×0.99 + 10 = 1990%; i.e., it falls.
- If $r>g$, the government must run a primary surplus – or else the ratio would (allegedly) march off to infinity. The primary surplus must be big enough so that subtracting it in Step 2 counters the compounding in Step 1. This is the case that all the debates are about.

Implausibility of an Ever-Rising Ratio

The possibility of the debt-to-GDP ratio rising to infinity is quite curious. If we were to take the model seriously, the economy would evolve such that interest payments are more than 100% of GDP. That is, bond holders receive more interest from the government than is needed to buy everything produced by the economy and put the excess income into buying more bonds.

This is an implausible outcome. Why would you want to hold more debt, when you can already buy everything within the economy? Instead, you might as well bid up the price of goods and services, so that you get a bigger portion of real output (remembering that it is extremely unlikely that all the debt is owned by a single individual, and that workers get incomes that will also want to buy goods and services). Formally, the propensity to consume out of wealth drops to zero, which appears to be the result of a pathological model.

Similar implausible outcomes that result from defective behavioural assumptions show up in more detailed analyses. Fullwiler describes the budgetary analysis of the American Congressional Budget Office (CBO) as follows:

> *In other words, a primary budget balance not at least as high as 0.6 percent of GDP on average would grow deficits, the national debt, and debt service all to the point that eventually paying the debt service would result in high and rising inflation. While this second row puts the convergence ratios at infinity for convenience, in fact at some point the increased debt service would simply pass through to inflation to raise nominal GDP in kind. Thus, CBO's regular practice of assuming a long-run nominal GDP growth rate equal to the potential real GDP growth rate plus inflation at around 2 percent is inconsistent with its own projections of unbounded growth in debt service payments.*

Fixing the Problem with SFC Models

As always, the problems with conventional analysis revolve around assumptions. In this case, the assumption that long-run GDP growth rates and interest rates are fixed (at "natural rates") makes little sense. If we look at stock-flow consistent (SFC) models (as discussed in my book *An introduction to SFC Models Using Python*), we see that SFC models do not exhibit such behaviour. An increase in government debt implies that private sector wealth is rising, and we should see increased consumption out of that wealth. If the increase in nominal demand is beyond the capacity of the economy to provide real goods and services, the price of goods and services would be bid higher. That is, the debt-to-GDP ratio would be inflated away by nominal GDP growing faster than the nominal interest rate.

In other words, the entire premise of debt sustainability analysis using this definition is based on obviously defective macroeconomic models. It is abundantly clear that the debt-to-GDP ratio will not go to infinity, rather the issue is the inflation risks posed by excessive aggregate demand.

Interest Rates Are a Policy Variable

Another important principle discussed in the Fullwiler article is the argument that the interest rates on government debt is a policy variable. (This debate was returned to in a 2020 article of his: "When the Interest Rate on the National Debt Is a Policy Variable (and 'Printing Money' Does Not Apply).")

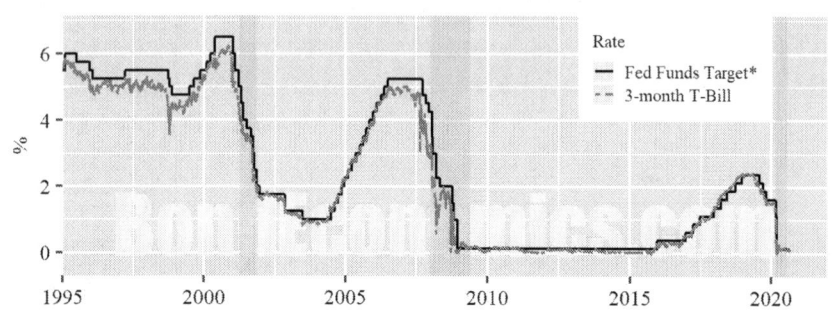

U.S. Short-Term Rates

Fed Funds And The 10-Year Yield

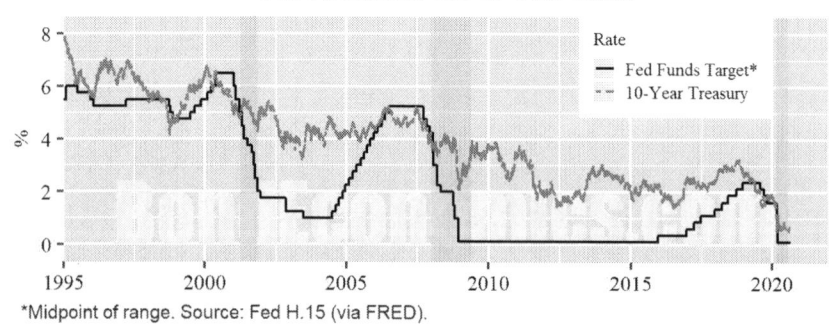

*Midpoint of range. Source: Fed H.15 (via FRED).

As the chart above shows, the 3-month Treasury bill rate is effectively glued to the Fed Funds target, while the level of the 10-year Treasury tends to be near the target. (I started the history in 1995 to roughly match the period of Fed transparency about the policy rate. The same story holds over longer periods.)

This is no accident. As Fullwiler noted in his second piece, short-term instruments like Fed funds, Treasury repurchase agreements ("repos"), and Treasury bills are money market instruments that all have the same credit risk – the U.S. Federal government. Small spreads open up for technical reasons (including the expectation of rate changes, as can be seen if one applies a magnifying glass to the Treasury bill history).

One could delve into the econometrics of the situation (as Fullwiler did) to validate there is a statistical relationship. The brute force analytical alternative is to observe the following: the U.S. government could just overhaul its operating procedures and stop issuing bills and notes – locking rates at zero. Yes, the payment of interest is a policy decision, not a law of nature.

Once we accept that the interest rate paid on debt is a policy decision, the entire discussion is a non-issue: just pay a rate of interest less than the growth rate, and the situation is always "sustainable"!

The neoclassical rebuttal is that although it looks like the Federal Reserve is free to set policy rates as they wish in any given meeting, they are forced to set the policy rate in a fashion to control inflation. For example, if they set the interest rate below the "correct" rate of inflation, then inflation will accelerate, and then the inflation-targeting mandate will eventually force even higher rates in the future. Whether they are constrained tightly is part of the debates between neoclassicals and MMT proponents about the effectiveness of interest rate policy (Section 2.5). I cannot hope to resolve that debate here.

One final note is that we see the problems with the neoclassical position (that neoclassicals generally attempt to obfuscate with terminology). The problem with "run-away debt" is almost certainly going to show up with increased demand from interest expenditures driving demand (otherwise we have the silliness of interest expenditures being larger than the economy). This interest rate/inflation spiral is only possible if the central bank keeps hiking rates – allegedly to control inflation!

Concluding Remarks

The analysis of fiscal sustainability is important, but it is done almost entirely within the framing chosen by conventional economists. The problem is that the framing makes no sense. As such, although the analysis is part of MMT, it is only there because of analytical errors by conventional economists.

References and Further Reading:
- "The debt ratio and sustainable macroeconomic policy," by Scott T. Fullwiler. *World Economic Review* 7 (2016): 12-42.
- "When the Interest Rate on the National Debt Is a Policy Variable (and 'Printing Money' Does Not Apply)," by Scott Fullwiler. Pre-print, 2020. URL: https://sci-hub.tw/downloads/2020-09-01/3c/10.1111@pbaf.12249.pdf

4.5 Theory of Inflation

The Monetary Monopoly Model (Section 4.3) is a core model of Modern Monetary Theory. If we take it literally, we do not need a theory of inflation, since the price level in some variants of the model is explicitly set as a policy variable. However, reality is far more complex than the model suggests, and if we want to match theory to reality, we are faced with the realisation that governments act in a fashion that sabotages the control of the price level that they do have.

The emphasis of this section is the discussion of theory that describes the current environment, with a short discussion of different policy choices.

The post-Keynesian view of the inflation process is that it is complex. There are no simple models that do a good job of fitting reality. This should be obvious to market practitioners – if a simple model did work, it would almost certainly have been found by people doing desperate searches across the set of time series inputs as well as the mathematical techniques to combine those inputs. One side effect of this complexity is that it does not appear that all MMTers will agree on the specifics, and so there is no simple "party line" to describe.

However, this complexity is missed completely by critics, who often invent their own theory of inflation that is attributed to MMT. The most ridiculous version of this I saw was an online assertion that "MMT is the Quantity Theory of Money, with bonds replacing money." This obviously does not work (the price level is not proportional to the stock of bonds), and unsurprisingly, there were no references to back the assertion.

Brief Discussion of Post-Keynesian Inflation Theory

The complexity of the inflation process has the implication that not everyone agrees on the details. Those details lie in what I refer to as broad MMT. Section 4.6 discusses broad MMT, as well as the splits among the various schools of thought within post-Keynesian economics. One would need to delve into these splits to get a better grasp of variant inflation theories. My explanation here is general, with the focus on what differentiates post-Keynesian thinking from neoclassical.

The first observation to make is that post-Keynesians distinguish between *flex price* and *administered* price, with flex price describing markets that somewhat resemble the simplified supply and demand stories of econom-

ics 101.
- A flex price market is one that is liquid and transparent, with many entities transacting, and prices changing rapidly. The clearest expression of these are financial markets, including auxiliary markets like wholesale commodity trading. Commodity trading is often done off exchanges, but often uses exchange pricing as a benchmark. Consumer prices are typically not flex price, but some qualify – gasoline prices being the most notable, but fresh fruits, vegetable, and meat being other contenders. Online markets that are not acting like traditional retailers also feature flexible prices. These markets are closest to matching the "supply and demand curve" story, but one needs to accept that market pricing is often based on highly variable sentiment (e.g., the spike then crash of oil prices in 2008). The wholesale futures markets are financial markets and have the odd behaviour that we have come to expect. However, the underlying fair value metric is normally thought of in terms of supply and demand in a broad sense. For example, crude oil futures (and some spot prices) in North America dropped to negative prices during the economic shutdown in 2020 once traders realised that there was no available storage to take delivery of oil contracts.
- Administered pricing is where the seller sets the price unilaterally, and then fills orders. Prices are normally set as a markup over costs, although there are many strategic choices to make (such as selling "loss leaders" at a low price to drive traffic to a store). The normal preference is to keep these administered prices stable, although some form of indexation can become common at higher inflation rates. The key point is the "supply and demand" curves or "equilibrium" does not appear in the description of the price-setting process.

Since real-world prices are set in a mixture of flex price and administered markets, aggregate price level determination is complex. For example, energy prices are key input to industrial prices, and can jump around based on sentiment about global growth (or cartel behaviour, as in the 1970s). Meanwhile, things like university tuition are set by administrators, and those administrators can make decisions that appear quite arbitrary.

As based on a response by Nathan Tankus to an initial draft of this text, at least some MMT proponents vigorously dislike the flex price/administrative terminology. However, since the canonical MMT textbook (as discussed next) distinguishes between domestic prices (presumably administered) versus imported raw materials prices (with international commodities and the exchange obviously flexible prices), there is a distinction between those two types of prices in the literature.

The next principle of post-Keynesian thinking is that inflation is a conflictual process, as discussed in Section 17.3 of Mitchell, Wray, and Watt's *Macroeconomics*. Those authors point to the line of authors going back to Michal Kalecki (a Marxist), who see inflation as the result of the struggle over real income. (To understand this, take a simplified model of the economy where everything is static, and all output is sold. The ratio of average wages to average output prices determines the share of output that is captured by workers; the remainder is consumed by capitalists that receive dividends from the profits. Bargaining between workers and firms set that ratio, and both sides wish to increase their share.)

The bargaining position of workers is generally better when the unemployment rate is low, as it is easier to quit. This obviously ends up similar to conventional stories about demand-driven inflation. The differentiating factor is that post-Keynesians view this as a power struggle, and not the result of prices being driven to marginal contributions of the factors of production. The neutering of labour power in the 1990s (Section 2.2) helps explain why inflation has been mild.

Cost-push inflation is another factor highlighted by Mitchell, Wray, and Watts, with raw material prices being particularly important. They write (page 258):

> *If in response to the fall in profit margin (mark-ups), domestic firms pass on the raw material cost increases in the form of higher prices, then workers would endure a cut to their real wages.*
>
> *If the workers resist this erosion of their real wages and push for higher nominal wage growth, then firms can either accept the squeeze on their profit margins or resist.*

They summarise the discussion of cost push and demand pull inflation as follows (page 261):

> *Cost push inflation requires certain aggregate demand conditions for it to be sustained. In this regard, it is hard to differentiate between an inflationary process which was initiated from supply side pressures from one that was initiated by demand side pressures.*

[Example of imported raw material price shock omitted.]
However, that conflict needs 'oxygen' in the form of ongoing economic activity in sectors where the spiral is robust. In that sense, the conditions that will lead to an accelerating inflation – high levels of economic activity – can also sustain an inflationary spiral emanating from the demand side.

The use of the word "sectors" in the last paragraph is important. It is entirely possible that some sectors are overheating – generating a wage-price spiral in those sectors – even while other sectors are weak and laying off workers. The widespread use of aggregate measures – like the overall unemployment rate – gives a misleading perspective on inflationary pressures in an economy. For this reason, simplified models are expected to fail when applied to real-world data.

From this perspective, one can see immediate problems with conventional price formation stories. Invoking supply and demand is largely an accounting identity or tautology – for every buyer, there is a seller. One needs to be able to come up with some mechanism for predicting price changes, and stories about marginal contributions do not fit real world experience. The reality that most prices are administered also explains why inflation and inflation expectations are linked – if firm managers expect rising input prices, they will raise their output prices. Therefore, the real question is, what determines those expectations? Do central bankers have the ability to unilaterally determine an arbitrary expected path of inflation – as suggested by some fundamentalist neoclassicals? Or are inflation expectations based on a holistic assessment of all government policies, as well as realised inflation?

More Distinctive MMT Inflation View?

If we want to draw a stronger distinction between MMT and other schools of thought within post-Keynesian economics, we need to look at discussions of alternative policies.
- The Job Guarantee offers the prospect of an anchor for nominal wages.
- Since inflation is often the result of bottlenecks, one widely-circulated article by Scott Fullwiler, Rohan Grey, and Nathan Tankus suggests using administrative means to deal with rising prices. (The difficulty in describing this approach is that institutional differences are large between countries. The medical and

educational systems in the United States have many inefficiencies that can be reduced, while other countries do not have such an abundance of low-hanging fruit.)
- The analysis of the failure of the NAIRU (Section 2.3) tells us what will not work – pretty well any model that uses a single aggregated unemployment rate as an explanatory variable for inflation. (Since employment is pro-cyclical by definition, and inflation under current institutional arrangements is also pro-cyclical, there will be a visual correlation on charts. However, this weak relationship does not offer much predictive power.)
- The microeconomic theory of Fred Lee discusses the logic behind administered pricing. The next section has a short description of this body of microeconomic thought.

However, if we want to discuss observed inflation, we have to accept that policymakers were not following policies suggested by MMT proponents. The modelling of the resulting inflation is complex, and from a qualitative standpoint, it is often hard to differentiate various views.

The rest of this section discusses more distinctive theories associated with MMT, and the difficulty in applying them to explain historical inflation.

The Monetary Monopoly Model

The Monetary Monopoly model does offer a simple explanation of how at least one price is set – it is determined as a policy choice. However, current government policy has been structured so that the government is a price taker in as many areas as possible (as suggested by conventional theory). However, the government does administer some prices, notably the wages of government employees (although public sector unions help determine the wage settlement). One argument is that government policies did accentuate the inflationary period that ended in the 1970s, which could be used as evidence for the theory. (This view is arguably controversial, and I do not want to be dragged into a debate about its validity.)

Within the current institutional environment, I am not convinced that changes requisitioning strategies alone can be used to fine tune the inflation rate (that is, do what inflation-targeting central banks allegedly achieve at present). A significant part of the basket of goods and services is largely driven by private sector trends, and it appears unlikely that doing something like fixing the prices paid for goods, services, and labour by the central government would be enough to damp out the relatively low inflation volatility that we have seen since the early 1990s. Instead, the government needs a programme with greater policy leverage, and the Job Guarantee provides that leverage. Although it should be clear that the previous statements are my opinion, one may note that the MMT literature generally discusses the Job Guarantee – or else regulatory/administrative changes (which step beyond what the Monetary Monopoly model suggests).

Functional Finance: A Story of Limits

Another source of confusion is the discussion of Functional Finance. The pertinent argument from Functional Finance is straightforward: the constraint on fiscal policy is inflation. However, this does mean that we can explain every wiggle of inflation by looking at fiscal variables. The following principles explain why this is so.

- Functional Finance argues that real resource constraints are the source of inflationary pressures, not nominal values. We cannot look at nominal deficit or debt levels and conclude anything about the fiscal stance. We would need to answer the more difficult question of what is happening with real resources.
- If the government is not forcing real constraints to be hit, we cannot say much about inflation based solely on government policy. The private sector still exists, and it can create inflationary pressures on its own.
- An alternative phrasing is that the process is nonlinear. For simplicity, assume that the economy is growing in a steady pace with a fiscal deficit of about 1% of GDP. Let us assume that a tax cut that increases the deficit by 10% of GDP (to 11%) would generate a surge in inflation. This does not imply that a tax cut that generates an increase in the deficit by 1% of GDP would imply an increase of one-tenth the size: if no resource constraints are hit, the modest increase in the deficit will be swamped by whatever else is going on in the economy. This nonlinearity means that we just cannot run regressions with fiscal variables versus inflation and expect them to be useful. Governments have not run fiscal policies that pushed real resource utilisation to extremes in decades, and so

one should expect historical correlations to be uninformative.

The argument from MMT proponents is that budgeting frameworks need to be overhauled to account for real resource bottlenecks. This was done in World War II. This task is not trivial, and will not just be a question of calculating a sensitivity between the inflation rate and the fiscal deficit.

No Easy Answers

As I discussed in Section 3.3 of *Breakeven Inflation Analysis*, forecasting inflation using a mathematical model is inherently challenging. The best results are short-term forecasts that are generated by finding the best model for each major component of the CPI, coupled with guesses about the direction of prices in energy markets (and similar). That said, such models are relatively useful for short-term breakeven inflation trading, but tell us little about inflation over longer horizons.

From a financial market practitioner's perspective, this should not be a surprise. Inflation is now a traded instrument, and if extremely accurate inflation models existed, the market would be rather boring. Whenever one is confronted with a reductionist model that allegedly predicts inflation, the first question to ask is: do inflation-linked traders use it? (The answer is almost invariably: no, they do not.)

As such, the MMT/post-Keynesian story that inflation is complex fits the facts on the ground rather well. A theory that offers a simple model of the inflation process is either tautological (just offers an alternative explanation of something that already happened) or wrong.

References and Further Reading
- *Macroeconomics*, by William Mitchell, L. Randall Wray, and Martin Watts. Red Globe Press, 2019. ISBN: 978-1-137-61066-9.
- "An MMT response on what causes inflation," by Scott Fullwiler; Rohan Grey, and Nathan Tankus. *FT Alphaville*, March 1, 2019. URL: https://ftalphaville.ft.com/2019/03/01/1551434402000/An-MMT-response-on-what-causes-inflation/

4.6 Broad MMT

The previous sections of this chapter (and earlier chapters) mainly revolved around what I term "narrow MMT." This is the distinctive theoretical core of

MMT, but it should be noted that the theory is fairly settled. Meanwhile, the academics associated with MMT continue to pursue research programmes, and hence the area covered by "MMT" continuously expands. This offends some critics, who insist that only some narrow set of principles constitutes MMT. Although it is entirely reasonable that someone would only be interested in the theoretical core of MMT, we need to accept that many MMT proponents view "MMT" as comprising the entire body of thought.

As one adds more theoretical content to MMT, the greater potential areas of controversy arise. If someone disagrees with the principles of "narrow MMT," it seems hard to classify them as an "MMT proponent." However, once we expand the range of theory, disagreements are likely to occur. There is no need to pursue doctrinal purity, so the reality that economists disagree should not be too troublesome. However, since this is a primer on "MMT," I need to offer some criteria to distinguish "MMT" from other schools of thought.

This text will only list a few references that I am familiar with; the reader can either use them to track down more, or use various online resources that list academic publications. The *Gower Initiative of Modern Money Studies* has created a large database of MMT academic articles: https://gimms.org.uk/tools-and-resources/

History of Money

One of the stranger developments in economics was the invention of the myth of barter. In "the old days," people allegedly used barter instead of money. (I will not expand upon this myth, since based on my experience, everyone is familiar with it.) Another set of myths about metallic coins is pushed by popular Austrian economists, who argue that anything other than gold-backed currencies is fraudulent (including fractional reserve banking).

Part of the Modern Monetary Theory research programme is an examination of these myths, putting an economic interpretation on earlier research by historians and anthropologists. The argument is that credit arrangements long pre-dated metallic coins. Chapters 2 and 3 of *Understanding Modern Money: The Key to Full Employment and Price Stability* by L. Randall Wray discuss the history of these debates, as well as how colonial powers introduced money via taxation.

Although historical wrangling is interesting, it has little to do with the analysis of macroeconomic dynamics in the twenty-first century. That said, this is one area of study that was undoubtedly advanced by MMT academics, and so it could be viewed as being part of the core of MMT.

Broad-Tent Post-Keynesian Economics

Marc Lavoie is a prolific author who has attempted to synthesise the various strands of post-Keynesian thinking into a coherent body of theory. In Section 1.4 of *Post-Keynesian Economics: New Foundations*, he outlined what he calls "broad-tent post-Keynesianism."

He divides post-Keynesian groups into a few strands:
- Fundamentalist Keynesians: Keynes himself, followed by other economists like Hyman Minsky, Paul Davidson, Jan Kregel, and the later writings of Joan Robinson.
- Kaleckians: those who are focused on questions of income distribution, with Michal Kalecki being the notable example.
- Sraffians: economists with an affinity to the topics pursued by Piero Sraffa. One of the key areas is the determination of relative prices within an economy.
- Institutionalists: economists with an interest in the underlying institutions of the economy (firms, monetary operations). Lavoie locates MMT within this strand.
- Kaldorians: economists with interests similar to Nicholas Kaldor's. Emphasis on growth and productivity, and the implications of international trade and transactions.

Unfortunately, one of the dominant characteristics of post-Keynesian economics is that it is largely defined by where it disagrees with neoclassical economics. This seems to attract contrary-minded economists, and the various groups of post-Keynesians are also split by interminable abstract theoretical debates. And the rise of MMT in the popular imagination has had the result that some post-Keynesians spend a considerable amount of time sniping at MMT. Since the post-Keynesians have read the scholarly output of MMT proponents, they unsurprisingly have stronger critiques than conventional economists, who quite often refuse to read the scholarly literature. (This aversion to reading journal articles raises the question of why so much attention is paid to publication counts within academia.) Furthermore, left-leaning post-Keynesians quite often target MMT proponents from the left (which might surprise people who believe MMT is socialism).

Section 5.8 delves further into post-Keynesian squabbling. However, it should be emphasised that the gap between post-Keynesian economics and neoclassical economics is much larger than the gap between MMT and other post-Keynesian groupings. From a practical perspective, any research programme carried on within the MMT or broad post-Keynesian tradition will end up in a very different place than one starting in the neoclassical tradition.

Stock-Flow Consistent (SFC) Models

Stock-flow consistent models are the preferred idiom for developing post-Keynesian models. The textbook *Monetary Economics: An Integrated Approach to Credit, Money, Income, Production and Wealth*, by Wynne Godley and Marc Lavoie is the standard textbook introduction. In addition to offering the best introduction to macroeconomics for people with a mathematical background, it has good textual explanations of the gaps between neoclassical thinking and post-Keynesian.

(My *An Introduction to SFC Models Using Python* offers a novel programming approach to the solution of these models, largely based on replicating the models in *Monetary Economics*. My text also outlines the differences in approaches.)

Legal Analysis

As one might expect from Institutionalists, considerable care is taken in the analysis of the legal framework of governmental finance. This is in contrast to the "assume something is true" strategy preferred by many conventional economists. The Trillion-Dollar Coin (Section 3.5) is probably the best-known implication of this research.

There has been some interest in MMT within law schools. This has meant that there is some wider legal analysis that draws on the MMT paradigm. One example is the paper "Mobile Finance in Developing Countries: Macroeconomic Implications and Potential" by Rohan Grey. This paper looks at the implications of the rise of electronic money. The rise of cryptocurrencies in popular discussion makes this a topic of interest.

Microeconomics

Modern Monetary Theory is often described as a macro theory, but the heterodox tradition also includes microeconomics. The late Frederic S. Lee was a prolific writer in microeconomics, and he taught at the University of Missouri at Kansas City (UMKC), alongside many prominent MMT academics.

I do not have much expertise in microeconomics, but after reading *Microeconomic Theory: A Heterodox Approach* (by Lee, edited by Tae-Hee Jo) I can offer the following comments relating Lee's research programme and MMT macroeconomics.

The first observation is that Lee's book offers an entire mathematical framework for modelling the economy, starting at the level of production of differentiated goods and services. Production is not some iron set of laws, it is rather the result of societal conventions. The question is how a society produces a surplus of goods and services that are used to meet the needs and desires of people. This framework is compatible with "Chartalist" notions of the nature of money. That is, this is an economic system that is compatible with macro formulations of narrow (core) MMT.

The next observation is that Lee contrasts and compares his approach to that used by those who follow in the tradition of Piero Sraffa. Based on my experience with heterodox academics, it seems that it is a safe bet that there are plenty of arcane theoretical disputes within post-Keynesian microeconomics.

That said, there is also a clear dividing line between Lee's exposition and neoclassical microeconomics. One issue is the argument that aggregation is misleading. This is not a trivial concern, since MMT proponents may refer to macro models that feature aggregated statistics. The explanation is straightforward: to what extent MMT proponents accept Lee's version of microeconomics, they are aware that the aggregated macro models are going to be approximations of reality that are expected to break down. This implies a greater need for cynicism with respect to mathematical economic models than to mainstream economists.

Given that neoclassical economics is currently based on micro-foundations (everything is the result of the aggregated optimising decisions of representative agents), it seems proper to argue that MMT needs its own micro-foundations.

Critiques of Neoclassical Economics

Neoclassical theory is normally developed in the form of mathematical models. The standard models are based on a variety of key behavioural assumptions. Within the body of post-Keynesian theory, every one of those assumptions is attacked as being unrealistic.

It should be noted that neoclassicals prolifically produce papers in which the various assumptions are relaxed and replaced with more sensible mechanics. However, the need for mathematical tractability means that only some assumptions can be worked with, and so the resulting model will still suffer from the other perceived defects.

This text concerns MMT, and not neoclassical theory. The question of whether the post-Keynesian critiques of neoclassical economics are correct is put aside. However, it should be noted that arguing that MMT proponents are incorrect because they are not taking into account some aspect of neoclassical theory is based on the assumption that neoclassical theory is correct – an assumption that MMT proponents do not share. A good faith critique would require responding to the objections to neoclassical theory first.

Political Economy and Interdisciplinary Studies
The interest in MMT is not confined to people who have an interest in monetary economics, the political economy implications have generated a wide following. The result is that if one goes to MMT conferences, there are presentations that are on topics that are associated with other branches of the humanities. For example, at the 2019 International MMT Conference, there was a session on racism, and one of the presentations that I found most memorable was on food banks.

Such discussions appear quite removed from the Monetary Monopoly Model, but they reflect the preference for multidisciplinary thinking in academia – which is resisted by the insular economics profession. The existence of such presentations makes suggestions that MMT proponents express "MMT" with a single mathematical model faintly ridiculous.

Concluding Remarks
Life would perhaps be simpler if one used a more generic label such as "post-Keynesian" or "heterodox" rather than "broad MMT" for describing the body of thought in question. However, such labelling does not match how many MMT proponents would define MMT (some might be satisfied with a definition that matches my description of narrow MMT).

The breadth of "broad MMT" implies that it cannot be easily summarised, as not everyone will agree with all points. This is different than narrow MMT, where if one disagrees, one would be classified as being a member of another school of thought. However, this broader set of knowledge is what will often come up in theoretical debates. The obvious risk is that "MMT" splits into theoretical factions, which I view as an unwelcome development.

References and Further Reading
- *Understanding Modern Money: The Key to Full Employment and Price Stability* by L. Randall Wray. Edward Elgar, 1998. ISBN: 978-1-84542-941-6
- *Post-Keynesian Economics: New Foundations,* by Marc Lavoie. Edward Elgar Publishing, 2014. ISBN: 978-1-78347-582-7
- *Monetary Economics: An Integrated Approach to Credit, Money, Income, Production and Wealth (Second Edition),* by Wynne Godley and Marc Lavoie. Palgrave-Macmillan, 2012. ISBN: 978-0-230-30184-9.
- "Mobile Finance in Developing Countries: Macroeconomic Implications and Potential," working paper, Rohan Grey. Found in the GIMMS Zotero paper database. URL: https://www.zotero.org/groups/2251544/mmt_academic_resources_-_compiled_by_the_gower_initiative_for_modern_money_studies/search/grey/titleCreatorYear/items/MEJ9CJ39/item-list
- *Microeconomic Theory: A Heterodox Approach,* by Frederic S. Lee, edited by Tae-Hee Jo. Routledge, 2018. ISBN: 978-0-367-35682-2.

Chapter 5 Frequently Raised Critiques

5.1 Introduction

Based on my experience, any mention of Modern Monetary Theory in an online environment will devolve into an argument. To reflect this reality, this chapter discusses some critiques of MMT that I have seen, which meet certain criteria (explained next). Normally, one might have a Frequently Asked Question (FAQ) in a text, but given the nature of online discourse, a Frequently Raised Critique (FRC) seems more appropriate. Since I consider myself in the MMT camp, I will explain to the best of my ability the MMT response. However, in most cases, my answers are not meant to be definitive rebuttals. Rather, one might need to go to other sources for more detailed responses to such critiques.

I cannot hope to cover all possible critiques, and I cannot claim to have the strongest possible statements of critiques. Furthermore, I think there is no way to usefully discuss some complaints, which I describe in the next section.

5.2 Non-Answerable Critiques

There are several ways of attacking MMT that are designed not to be answered. Whether the reader finds them convincing depends almost purely on personal preferences.

- An MMT supporter on the internet said something wrong.
- Well-known MMT proponents said something that is incorrect.
- If we assume that MMT is incorrect, then MMT is false.
- Critics get to define what MMT is.
- Just don't like the politics.

MMT Supporter on the Internet Was Wrong!
There are many MMT activists on the internet, and they are not afraid of letting people know what they think (I fall into this category).

Unfortunately, many are not experienced with economic discussion, and can misinterpret MMT, and/or not understand the responses of the people they are arguing with. It is unsurprising that they will periodically write something indefensible. Although this is bad advertising for MMT, nobody should be surprised that somebody said something wrong on the internet. That is why academics write long-form content in peer-reviewed journals or books.

One genre of arguments revolves around triumphalist statements by MMT supporters, where they contrast MMT to other economic theories. In many cases, those statements would require qualifications. There is no doubt that hyperbole by MMT supporters is going to aggravate people who sympathise with other schools of thought. That said, whether or not MMT supporters characterise other economic theories correctly is a distraction from discussing MMT, which is my focus herein.

Well-Known MMT Proponent Was Wrong About Something!

People who like writing about economics tend to like to write about economic events. Given a large enough set of statements on current economic controversies, it seems extremely likely that bad forecasts will be made. Meanwhile, MMT proponents are economists, and are subject to the occupational hazard of not agreeing with each other. Unless we want to fragment MMT into multiple versions, one person cannot speak for the entire school of thought.

Expecting every MMT proponent to be always correct about everything is a standard that no school of thought could expect to meet. Once again, that is why academics write long-form articles and books – to allow for careful debate, and hopefully expose errors of thinking.

If We Assume MMT Is Incorrect, It Is False!

One common strategy is to dismiss MMT because some aspect of it contradicts an existing result within conventional economics.

Such a critique of MMT could be quite devastating – but it is reliant on that aspect of conventional theory being correct. Since a good portion of post-Keynesian thought consists of attacking every aspect of mainstream economics, it is almost certainly true that there is an existing rebuttal to the argument. One would need to delve into the critique of conventional theories, which is normally skipped over.

MMT Is What I Say It Is!

Some high-profile critics have created straw-man versions of MMT, and then attacked that straw man. The description of MMT bore no resemblance to actual MMT doctrine. As was predictable, other critics read these criticisms, and spread the misrepresentations.

It is easy to pick out such critiques: there is no citation of MMT sources, but rather those of MMT critics. Quite often, the "summary" of MMT involves stating the opposite of the MMT stance.

These complaints are extremely common in popular discourse, as they appear to be the result of people repeating someone else's fictional version of MMT.

Don't Like the Politics!

Finally, many critics do not like the politics of MMT. Normally, this comes from free market leaning conventional economists, but they are joined by groups like the Sound Finance Socialists. Political complaints are important, but not ones that are within the scope of this book (as discussed in Section 1.3).

Non-Answerable Critiques Are Extremely Common

These complaints capture a significant portion of popular MMT critiques, including those made by senior academics. Correspondingly, there are many high-profile criticisms (e.g., book reviews by high profile academics) that are skipped over here, since they fall into this category.

5.3   Rhetorical Tricks (and Money Printing)

Critics quite often complain about rhetorical tricks used by MMT proponents, or alternatively, that meanings of words are being twisted. Given that MMT academics have aimed to shift the terminology used in discussing fiscal policy, this is somewhat to be expected.

I think it is safe to make the following two observations with respect to this issue.

1. Some conventional phrasings used with respect to fiscal and monetary policy are misleading and are designed to slant debate in a certain direction. The terminology is not politically neutral, and so the MMT objections are justifiable.
2. Some people have been confused by the alternative terminology used by MMT proponents. However, this is not universal; I was introduced to MMT via contact with the writings of the original MMT exponents, and I found the writings perfectly clear.

The second point is obviously a concern. I can see several reasons for

the confusion.
- The reality is that people skim when reading. If one has already fixed notions about economics, it is entirely possible to misunderstand a passage explaining an alternative viewpoint, particularly if novel terminology is used. This is a good faith misunderstanding of text, and to be expected for a novel theory.
- My view is that certain prominent MMT critics have deliberately misrepresented MMT when attacking it. These misrepresentations are then repeated by others, creating a fog of misinformation around the topic.
- In popular discussions, pro-MMT writers have given incorrect explanations of MMT principles. This could be chalked up to either not understanding the original point, or their inexperience with the subject leading them to give a mangled explanation.
- Texts are written using preferred MMT idioms, and the meaning can be misinterpreted if one is unfamiliar with the terminology. This is the case that some critics are arguing is the problem.

With respect to the last point, I accept that some passages could easily be misinterpreted. That said, critics often have a hard time pinpointing actual passages that are a problem. If one reads the academic arguments in context, meanings are typically quite clear.

The rest of this section discusses a couple examples of semantic discussions.

Money Printing

Scott Fullwiler's article "When the Interest Rate on the National Debt Is a Policy Variable (and 'Printing Money' Does Not Apply)" has a lengthy digression on the lack of understanding around the phrase "printing money." This is in reference to the long-running debate about the details of governmental finance, as well as the MMT objections to conventional framing.

The early MMT literature proved difficult for many scholars to grasp. The crude, now popularized view of MMT as simply "printing money" suggests little has changed. While a critic's background in economics has never been strongly correlated with correctly interpreting MMT literature, enough scholars did correctly interpret MMT that a noncynical take is that critics' difficulties arose from the fundamental shift in thinking MMT (especially in its earliest years) required of readers.

He then moves to argue that there is no simple way to summarise

MMT, as the discussion of monetary operations is complex, and requires a great many steps. (Critics often spent a good amount of time quibbling about details in those steps.) He returns to "printing money" later.

Ultimately, they might have asked what exactly MMT meant by "printing money" given MMT's frequent declarations that all deficits, however "financed," were "printing money." If the government runs a deficit and also sells a bond for the same amount and MMT nevertheless calls this "printing money," it is obvious that MMT is saying something different from what is normally meant by "printing money." Any academically rigorous critique of MMT should demonstrate such a basic understanding.

He then asks: "What *does* [emphasis in original] MMT mean, then, by 'printing money?'" The explanation runs over six paragraphs, ending with:

What matters is the deficit. Thus, for MMT, "printing money" means the creation of additional net financial assets for the private sector, which every deficit does, whether a bond is sold or not.

I do not feel that I can summarise those six paragraphs without being part of the confusion problem. I would instead offer this explanation, which (I believe) is consistent with MMT, and hard to misinterpret. Rather than attempting to reframe the terminology, just re-state the issues.

1. The conventional usage of terms like "printing money" is hopelessly confused, and the Economics 101 textbook story that spending is "financed by taxes, bond issuance, and money creation" is either trivial or incorrect. If we ignore this framing, most of our problems disappear.
2. By an accounting identity, if government expenditures (of all types) are greater than monetary inflows in an accounting period, the government must issue liabilities of the corresponding amount. (If the government used private bank accounts, a correction for their change would need to be added. However, central government usage of private banks is generally insignificant in modern developed countries.)
3. The means of emission of governmental liabilities is country-specific and mired in institutional and legal details. The *only* interesting aspect of this to most people is whether there is a chance of a governmental default on its liabilities. The answer will depend upon legal analysis – and none of these legal

theories have been tested in court. My view of the consensus of serious government bond analysts was that there was negligible risk of an *involuntary* default for the non-Euro developed countries. (Governments can voluntarily repudiate debt. I discuss this in Section 6.6 of *Understanding Government Finance*.)
4. MMT proponents argue that the issuance of money *must* precede its return to government via taxes or bond issuance. This logical point is given considerable weight in discussions. I am heretical with regards to the MMT consensus in that I am concerned that this point can lead to largely semantic debates. I prefer to emphasise default risk analysis that results from operations analysis.
5. The exact mix of governmental liabilities that are outstanding is a function of private sector asset allocation decisions (which are affected by regulations). For example, the number of banknotes in circulation is mainly driven by the desire of the private sector to use them in small retail transactions (and illegal activity). If the government decided to make payments using banknotes, the banknotes would almost immediately be returned to the consolidated government via the banking system. As such, the government does not control the mix of "money" or "debt" in its liabilities. This is a feature of the real world, as well as post-Keynesian and *neoclassical* models. In other words, anyone who is numerate will not frame governmental financing as a question of whether the government issues debt or money.

I will let the reader decide whether attempts to change the conventional framing about money creation and the financing operations of central governments has been successful or not. My suggestion is to stick to concrete questions – and to be suspicious of Economics 101 wisdom.

Affordability

One recent example of a complaint about rhetoric was in Matthew C. Klein's review of Stephanie Kelton's The Deficit Myth ("MMT's Stephanie Kelton Advocates for Permanent Wartime Economics"):

> Kelton sometimes relies on sleight of hand to make her case. She rightly notes that the government is financially unconstrained when it comes to paying Medicare beneficiaries, for example, because it can't run out of money. But that doesn't tell us whether Medicare is sustainable as currently struc-

tured. Population aging, trends in obesity, and the persistent increase in the relative cost of healthcare all mean that Medicare will, on its current trajectory, end up eating more of the rest of society's resources. Elsewhere, Kelton suggests the answer is to shift more and more of the workforce into medicine and elder care. But that's quite different from saying that "the biggest challenges facing these programs have nothing to do with affordability."

I see two legs to these statements: the substantive policy concerns, and then the narrow question is whether there is a rhetorical trick.

With regard to the substantive policy issues around Medicare in the United States, it is entirely plausible that it will take increasing amounts of real resources as the population ages. Whether this increase of resources can be easily dealt with – and how to deal with it – is obviously open to debate. Since my concern was more with the Canadian debate than the American one, I have no strong opinions on that subject.

Instead, the disagreement is whether saying this has "nothing to do with affordability" is a "rhetorical trick." I will first note that the substantive issue is that this is a question of real resources, and Klein's description of the problem matches this. I would argue that there are many linguistic precedents for treating real resource constraints as not being an issue of "affordability."

Since everyone loves household analogies, I will use one. Imagine that we have cooked supper for our family, but. I then discover that one of my children has invited friends over to eat at the last minute. There is a definite concern that we might run out of prepared food, but there is no question of our being able to "afford" the extra food – unless these friends have extremely large appetites. So, we have a real resource constraint, but not an affordability constraint, and that is how people use the word "affordability" in the real world.

So why is discarding "affordability" seen as a rhetorical trick? I would guess that this is the result of conventional economists framing resource limits as being about "affordability." By extension, if one denies that "affordability" is not a concern, the argument is that one could leave the impression that you are saying there are no real resource constraints either. Although there is a logic to that, it is puzzling to me that one would complain that MMT proponents are using words *correctly*.

Concluding Remarks

There are other examples of the complaint of word-twisting, but in most cases, I am unconvinced about the good faith of the critics in question. All I can suggest is to keep in mind that MMT proponents have targeted changing the framing used in economics, and so one needs to be careful in interpreting what they write. However, if one reads entire texts – and not rely on out-of-context quotes – I do not think this a particular challenge.

References and Further Readings

- "When the Interest Rate on the National Debt Is a Policy Variable (and 'Printing Money' Does Not Apply)," by Scott Fullwiler. Pre-print, 2020. URL: https://sci-hub.tw/downloads/2020-09-01/3c/10.1111@pbaf.12249.pdf
- Matthew C. Klein: "MMT's Stephanie Kelton Advocates for Permanent Wartime Economics," *Barron's*, June 5, 2020. URL: https://www.barrons.com/articles/the-case-for-permanent-wartime-economics-51591355446

5.4 Need to Lie to Politicians and Voters

One relatively common complaint that I have seen is that Modern Monetary Theory should be ignored because fiscal policymakers cannot be trusted to control inflation. This might be called the "noble lie" critique: we need to avoid discussing MMT as policymakers might make "undesirable" decisions.

This is obviously a political economy concern, related to the perennial "is MMT socialist?" debate (Section 1.2). The other issue with this critique is that this is obviously referring to a narrow definition of MMT (the parts that are related to Functional Finance). Since most online arguments about MMT are about those parts of MMT, this narrow scope matters, but as I argued in Section 1.2, that is missing too much of MMT for anyone interested in economic theory.

The remarks here are based upon the article "Modern Monetary Muddle," by Michael Edesess. This article was a review of Stephanie Kelton's book *The Deficit Myth*. I have seen many variants of this complaint elsewhere, but often shorter and harder to discuss. Edesess' critique could be related to arguments made by neoclassical economists about fiscal policy, which I defer to a technical appendix.

Edesess' Arguments

Within his review of *The Deficit Myth*, Edesess argues that the arguments of many prominent MMT critics – Martin Wolf, John H. Cochrane, Larry Summers, and Paul Krugman (a bipartisan group) – come down to a similar theme. The theme is that the critics agree with the analytical premises of MMT, but are concerned about its effect on policy. Edesess argues:

> *But there is an even more basic issue raising those fears. They don't trust Congress to make the appropriate adjustments. Would Congress, observing that - or being advised that - the economy was overheating therefore raise taxes to mop up the excess dollars, as MMT advocates? [another scenario]*
>
> *No, they don't trust Congress to do that - in fact they don't trust democracy to do it. And for good reason.*
>
> *Democracy has a Tragedy of the Commons problem. A Tragedy of the Commons is, for example, a fish pond shared by many anglers, each of which, in their own self-interest, catches as many fish as they can, with the unfortunate collective result that the pond gets fished out.*
>
> *[...]*
>
> *Any threat to that arrangement is dangerous. To keep the unwashed masses from prevailing upon - or electing - a government that tries to provide all things to all people, as in a populist state, we must perpetuate the fiction that all new expenditures must be immediately paid for by new taxes. And we must delegate the management of the supply of money not to a democratic process, but to a quasi-authoritarian government arm, the Fed.*

I do not think that Edesess' analogy to the "tragedy of the commons" is persuasive (he discusses it further in the article), it sounds like an Economics 101 story stretched beyond its breaking point. The neoclassical arguments I allude to in the technical appendix is the more rigorous version of the argument. Instead, the value of the argument is that Edesess explicitly writes out the political economy argument: the "unwashed masses" need to be controlled by the "quasi-authoritarian" central bank.

There seems to be two main reasons to be interested in MMT: an interest in economic theory, or policy. I discuss these in turn.

Economic Theory Perspective

The argument that policymakers might behave badly is a complete non-issue from the perspective of economic theory. I am not going to believe something is nonsensical just because someone might misuse the knowledge. From an academic perspective, this trivially does need elaboration.

The only interesting aspect is that I would guess that many people feel that theory ought to be tied to advocacy. This is extrapolating the norms of financial market analysis. For example, loudmouth free market fundamentalists predicting the demise of either the Japanese or American bond market is a perennial source of popular headlines. (Financial media editors know that fiscal crisis stories catch more attention, and that retail investors are otherwise not very interested in bond markets.)

However, this behavioural norm is not universal. Attention-seeking fund managers or strategists may very well be in the minority. For example, when I was an analyst, it was expected that I would not offer any useful information about a fund's positioning to outsiders. (The easiest way of doing this is professing ignorance of practically everything.)

If one does not broadcast one's views about fiscal policy, what they are will have no effect on politicians. As such, this entire line of enquiry is a non-starter.

Policy Perspective

If we are interested in how policy is structured, we have a plausible reason to be concerned about policy biases.

The first thing to note is that the discussion of a fiscal policy bias means that we are only discussing the parts of MMT that are related to it. This means that we are stuck with an extremely narrow definition of MMT – that is even narrower than what I describe as "narrow MMT." So even if we accept Edesess' argument, it is not really discussing all of the theory.

The problem with the argument is that we are stuck in a rather unusual situation (which Edesess acknowledges). The MMT argument is that the only constraint on fiscal policy is inflation – and that fiscal policy frameworks should be based upon that premise. It is hard to see how that is inherently inflationary.

For this critique to be not obviously wrong, we need to re-phrase it. Instead, the argument could be that MMT proponents are not analysing inflation risks properly, and that they have a bias towards policies that could lead to inflation. This is a legitimate area of debate, and I will return to the question of inflation control in Section 5.5.

Otherwise, we are stuck arguing about the motivation of and the competence of MMT proponents. Although some people will enjoy doing this, this does not really tell us much about the *theory*.

Finally, the argument that only central bankers are defending the soundness of the currency does not reflect current political reality. Among the population, inflation is politically unpopular. Meanwhile, the post-2008 era has seen various developed central bankers pleading with politicians to loosen fiscal policy. Some left-leaning economists are defending the creation of independent fiscal watchdogs to prevent the repeat of post-crisis austerity episodes. (I think this is a mistaken view, but it is a signal about the perceived biases of politicians in the real world.)

Technical Appendix: Time Consistency

One of the big ideas of neoclassical modelling of the 1970s was time consistency of policies. This was part of the ideological attack on Keynesianism, as it was argued that fiscal policy was time inconsistent. Since I am not writing a primer on neoclassical economics, I will keep this description short.

Imagine that policymakers want to reduce unemployment while keeping inflation stable. We assume that the framework is Old Keynesian: increase government spending to create jobs (or cut taxes), but the rise in aggregate demand creates inflationary pressures.

(This framework ignores the Job Guarantee, which features full employment at a fixed policy wage. Jackson Mejia and Brian C. Albrecht released an initial analysis of time consistency when applied to MMT, but I had technical concerns about the treatment. The pre-print could easily be revised by the time you read this, so there is no point in going into details. The reader may be able to find an updated version, which would be one of the earlier serious neoclassical analyses of MMT. Please note that my description here is a simplified version of the old-time consistency arguments, and may not reflect that paper.)

The time inconsistency shows up in the following fashion. Assume that unemployment is "too high," and so policymakers want to launch a fiscal stimulus programme. They argue that future fiscal tightening will offset future inflation risks, so that the mixed policy objective is met. However, in the following year, unemployment is at a more comfortable level, and inflation is higher, as policy was not tightened by as much predicted.

Within the model, this effect happens because the policy setting in a period is the result of an optimisation problem based upon the current situation, and the expected future. What happened in the past no longer matters. The result is that the optimal solution in the first year predicts a fiscal tightening in the second year, to balance out the inflation and unemployment objectives. However, when re-running the optimisation in the second year, the inflation/unemployment situation in the first year is no longer considered, and so the new policy mix is looser than forecast. The result is the resulting policy mix has a greater bias towards inflation.

This story is not just an analogy picked out of an Economics 101 textbook, rather it is a model aimed at this policy concern. That said, the obvious rebuttal is that MMT proponents are aware of the time consistency literature and reject the various assumptions that go into those models. That discussion is well beyond the desired complexity of this text, so I will not attempt to dig any deeper.

References and Further Readings
- "Modern Monetary Muddle," by Michael Edesess, a review of Stephanie Kelton's *The Deficit Myth*. URL: http://econintersect.com/pages/opinion/opinion.php?post=202007020028
- The following pre-print updates the time consistency literature and discusses MMT. Mejia, Jackson, and Brian C. Albrecht. "Time Inconsistency, Inflation, and MMT." (2020). URL: https://briancalbrecht.github.io/Mejia_Albrecht_MMT.pdf

5.5 Inflation Worries

One of the basic premises of Functional Finance is that real resource constraints are the only ones faced by floating currency sovereigns and hitting those resource constraints typically results in inflation. As such, MMT proponents argue that the budgeting process should revolve around inflation control, and not nominal debt levels.

Therefore, it seems somewhat curious that online critics often base their attacks on MMT on inflation risks – or in many cases, hyperinflation. In my view, most of those attacks tell us more about the psychology of MMT critics than MMT. However, there are some lines of criticism that appear defensible. If one wanted to have good faith discussions of MMT policy proposals, inflation control ought to be of primary concern – which is exactly what the theory suggests.

Hyperinflation Hyperbole

Anyone who has read a lot of financial market commentary (as well as online economic arguing) will realise that hyperinflation in modern developed economies is discussed many more times than there are actual incidents in these countries (zero). Even highly credentialled neoclassical economists dip into hyperinflation fearmongering. For example, in "A Skeptic's Guide to Modern Monetary Theory," N. Gregory Mankiw writes:

> *Faced with these circumstances, a government may decide that defaulting on its debts is the best option, despite its ability to create more money. That is, government default may occur not because it is inevitable but because it is preferable to hyperinflation.*

To my eyes, the suggestion that hyperinflation is an outcome that a developed floating currency sovereign would face is highly implausible, and the burden is upon the person invoking hyperinflation to come up with an explanation of how it could occur. To date, I have never seen a critic tackle that question in a serious way.

The rest of this section will discuss serious criticisms of MMT's perspective on inflation handling.

A Floating Currency…Floats

One popular concern is about the value of the domestic currency in foreign exchange markets. Given that the MMT policy preference is for floating exchange rates, and that the entire premise of floating exchange rates is that the value of the currency in foreign exchange markets floats, I am somewhat bewildered by these concerns.

I will return to this issue in Section 5.10, but I just want to note that we cannot conflate inflation with a drop in the value of the domestic currency versus foreign ones. Inflation refers to the evolution of domestic prices, and not what foreign goods you can buy with your home currency.

Job Guarantee: One Way Stabilisation?

One straightforward argument I have run across is that the Job Guarantee will only stop deflation in wages, but it has limited power to stop wages from rising. (I have seen this argument in online discussions, but I did not have a useful source to quote.)

It is easy to see how deflation is prevented: the private sector cannot easily pay a lower wage than the Job Guarantee wage (JG wage for short). If the private sector is shrinking, workers will be laid off and end up earning the JG wage, growing the fiscal deficit. This will put a floor under nominal demand, allowing the economy to recover.

What happens when the economy overheats?
Even if some employers have reservations about hiring workers from the JG pool, they probably also have a reservation against giving pay raises. So long as the JG pool has workers that are considered employable, it seems likely that they would be drawn into the private sector instead of employers bidding up wages to poach employees from other firms. (Given the exclusionary employment practices seen in the past, the phrase "considered employable" does have awkward implications.)

However, at some point, the Job Guarantee would be emptied of workers who are considered employable. At that point, the JG pool does not act as a deterrent against across-the-board private sector wage increases. (Realistically speaking, wages for specialised workers would rise before the JG pool was empty – which implies that wage dispersion/inequality would increase.)

Although that sounds problematic, we have to keep in mind that this scenario implies literally full employment. The only workers who qualify as unemployed are those who are transitioning between jobs. This would be viewed as an impressive achievement, as under conventional analysis, this is the maximum output achievable.

Nevertheless, we need to remember the base premise of Chartalism: taxation drives the value of the currency. The Job Guarantee helps anchor the wage price level, but it is not sufficient – taxes are needed. Income taxes are progressive – even flat tax systems since what they include is a threshold income below which income is not taxed. As wages rise, the tax take increases, and acts to modulate growth. As such, the entire fiscal programme needs to be taken into account, and not just the Job Guarantee.

The interesting debate is whether the Job Guarantee wage will help anchor wage settlements in the private sector. If it does (as suggested by MMT proponents), inflation performance should improve, since there is a stronger signal about the desired price structure in the economy. However, resolving whether this is correct or not is entirely dependent upon guesswork in the absence of the implementation of a full-scale Job Guarantee. (Doing an experiment in some small town is not going to prove very much.) It goes without saying that MMT proponents and mainstream economists differ on how to do the guesswork.

Is the Inflation Constraint Measurably Different than "Financial" Constraints?

One possibility that critics dance around (but I cannot recall seeing explicitly) is the possibility that the "inflation constraint" ends up in practice as coinciding with a "financial constraint." For example, it is possible that one could develop a rule that suggests that there is a limit for fiscal deficits that can be safely run without inflation risk. This argument certainly appears to align with the mental models used by MMT critics.

The reason to doubt this argument is that one can point to various post-1990 episodes of fiscal expansion that worried conventional economists – yet there was no inflationary impact. (The most notable being the post-Financial Crisis situation, while the Japanese situation mocked the hyperinflationists.) The other major concern is that this would suggest that long-term inflation forecasting is relatively easy, while in practice it seems difficult to do across different economic regimes.

Nevertheless, even if one can find such a rule, the theoretical argument – that inflation matters, not financing – still holds.

References and Further Readings
- "A Skeptics Guide to Modern Monetary Theory," N. Gregory Mankiw, presentation to AEA meeting, January 2020. URL: https://scholar.harvard.edu/files/mankiw/files/skeptics_guide_to_modern_monetary_theory.pdf

5.6 Active Fiscal Policy Required?

Another argument I have seen is that Functional Finance (and the locking of interest rates at 0%) implies a need to continuously adjust fiscal policy to control inflation. This is by analogy to monetary policy, where central banks have policy meetings at a relatively high frequency (for example, eight times a year).

This criticism is distinct from a similar-sounding criticism that governments will be slow to hike taxes in response to higher inflation. That is the time consistency critique, discussed in the previous section. The concern here is the disruption caused by rapid tax changes.

I do not have a particular critic to quote for this complaint, but it is a reasonable argument. It does not seem controversial to argue that it would be disruptive if tax rates were changed every few months.

The immediate response to this criticism is that I am unaware of any MMT proponents who advocate continuous changes to fiscal policy setting to fine-tune inflation. Instead, automatic stabilisers are advocated (such as the Job Guarantee). The premise of automatic stabilisers is that fiscal policy will tend to stabilise nominal incomes, even with fixed fiscal policy settings.

It is not only spending programmes (like the Job Guarantee) that act as automatic stabilisers; taxes are specified as being a rate imposed against nominal income or spending (in the case of a value-added tax). Even if nothing is changed, the fiscal balance rises and falls with the cycle.

Another response is that administrative controls can be used, which I will discuss at the end of this section. Such measures can help stabilise inflation rates, but I would not expect them to be sufficient to offset extremely loose (or tight) fiscal policy.

Lump Sum Taxes?

One reason why continuous tax changes are allegedly needed is the use of lump sum taxes in simple economic models. A lump sum tax is a tax where the government levies a fixed amount (as in the Monetary Monopoly Model described in Section 4.3). To implement such a tax, a flat amount per person would be levied.

The amount taxed is invariant to the state of the cycle, and so it would need to be adjusted continuously if it were to be used in active control of the economy. As such, anyone who uses such a model will conclude that fiscal policy is an awkward stabilisation tool.

The problem is that real-world taxes are mainly paid on nominal flows (income, sales), with a small amount of property taxes (and other user fees). The tax take will adjust with the cycle automatically.

Answer Depends Upon Disputed Theory

Automatic stabilisers are not enough to stabilise the economy on their own; they have been in existence since the end of World War II, yet recessions still happen. (In fact, recessions have been less frequent since the 1990s, and by most accounts, automatic stabilisers have been weakened.)

The conventional argument is that monetary policy has been key to regulating the economy, keeping inflation near target, and recessions less frequent. As was discussed in Section 2.5, MMT disputes that view, instead suggesting that monetary policy is not particularly effective.

It is straightforward that resolving that debate will tell us whether fiscal policy would need to be activist to stabilise the economy. *My* argument is that monetary policy did not accomplish too much in the post-1990 era (other than inflating housing bubbles), and fiscal policy settings were relatively stable in most developed countries (with some exceptions, such as crisis responses). This suggests that we have a historical period to point to where inflation was relatively stable, in the absence of activist fiscal policy (putting aside the inevitable crisis responses).

Better Budgeting Helps

Another factor to keep in mind is that fiscal policy is meant to take inflation risks into account. Even if the bulk of the budget is largely on autopilot, discretionary spending still exists. It would not be a good idea to modulate that spending on a monthly basis (which is theoretically possible for monetary policy), but it could still be moved in line with medium-term economic developments. Given that monetary policy is normally moved in a smooth fashion as well, this responsiveness is still comparable to monetary policy.

Administrative Inflation Control

Administrative controls are an alternative to using fiscal and monetary policies to control inflation. This could be either wage and price controls, or perhaps planning techniques used to reduce bottlenecks that lead to inflation.

Section 17.5 of the textbook *Macroeconomics* by Mitchell, Wray, and Watts discusses income policies. Wage and price controls were quite common in developed countries up until the 1960s. The record of wage and price controls was mixed in the United States, but the authors argue that they were successful in the Scandinavian model.

Nevertheless, they note that income policies fell out of favour in the 1970s, as a consequence of the rise of Monetarism.

Researchers in the MMT tradition argue that we can go beyond the experience of earlier decades. The article "An MMT Response on what Causes Inflation" by Scott Fullwiler, Rohan Grey, and Nathan Tankus was a high-profile entry in the argument that administrative controls can be used to control inflation. They argue that the issue is bottlenecks in production, and not just aggregate demand issues.

> *Regardless of which policy tool is used in a particular context, demand management in general needs to lean much more heavily on the appearance of bottlenecks in specific industries instead of simply tracking changes in a general price index. The immediate signs of bottlenecks are large and sustained rises in unfilled orders for specific goods and services. Preventing shortages is after all what demand management is first and foremost about and price indices are misleading policy targets when they include factors that are insensitive to demand and would be counterproductive to manage with demand. The more actively we regulate big business for public purpose, the tighter the full employment we can achieve and the more resources we can devote to the Green New Deal while preserving price stability.*

In my view, there is one easy way to market the argument – the government needs to avoid being part of the source of inflationary problems. It should conduct its operations in such a way to help control prices. Commerce is conducted within a legal framework, and that framework should have inflationary consequences in mind.

Nevertheless, I am not hugely enthusiastic about the approach. It would be an obvious political challenge trying to market rebranded wage and price controls. Once we move beyond that, we are stuck with the problem that the approach is dependent upon local legal institutions. Even if a policy works in one country, it might not transplant to another.

Credit Controls

Credit controls are administrative measures to control lending growth and could be viewed as an alternative version of monetary policy. Given the importance of the residential housing market to aggregate demand, and the reality that household mortgages are generally under stricter regulations than business borrowing, this is an obvious avenue to be explored. (For example, Canada has considerable control over the housing market via the use of its regulations around mortgage insurance. Mortgage insurance is required for all mortgages with a down payment of less than 20% of property value. Changes to the qualifications for insurance helped fuel the national housing bull market that started in the late 1990s.)

Attempting to regulate business borrowing is trickier, as there is a large industry of bankers, lawyers, and accountants working in financial centres whose job description is to help businesses "arbitrage" regulations (and taxes). The U.S. Government is used to throwing its weight around, but it is unclear whether a small country like Canada could make such regulations stick.

Concluding Remarks

If policymakers push economies back to tighter labour markets, inflation control would be more challenging than it is at present. As the 1970s showed, inflation control is not trivial. That said, avoiding the mistakes made by the old Keynesian aggregated framework is a good place to start.

References and Further Reading
- *Macroeconomics,* by William Mitchell, L. Randall Wray, and Martin Watts. Red Globe Press, 2019. ISBN: 978-1-137-61066-9.
- "An MMT Response on what Causes Inflation" by Scott Fullwiler, Rohan Grey, and Nathan Tankus. *FT Alphaville*, March 1, 2019. URL: https://ftalphaville.ft.com/2019/03/01/1551434402000/An-MMT-response-on-what-causes-inflation/

5.7 MMT Ignores the Banking System?

Over the years, I have seen criticisms that MMT somehow ignores the banking system, and the role of banks in creating money within the economy. In my view, this is at best a semantic argument about the tone of online primers. The critic believes that more emphasis should be placed on bank money creation, whereas the authors of MMT primers disagree. I have no interest in policing the tone of publications, so I do not have too much sympathy for such debates.

J.W. Mason Review Comments

I am going to use as an example a comment J.W. Mason made in a review of Stephanie Kelton's *The Deficit Myth* (URL: https://prospect.org/culture/books/mmt-can-we-create-all-the-money-we-need/). Mason writes:

> The big weakness is the book's central theoretical claim that government has a monopoly in money creation, a theory known as "chartalism." This claim has a serious problem: the existence of banks. It is true that government has a monopoly on currency. But most of the money we use in our daily lives is not coins and bills issued by the government, but ledger entries created by banks. Banks are money issuers every bit as much as the government. Government has tools to influence how

much money is created by private banks, but its control isn't absolute. And when its control is effective, that's a function of the regulations and institutions of the financial system; it has nothing to do with the government monopoly on currency.

Since *The Deficit Myth* is a popular book, we should not expect it cover every theoretical dispute within post-Keynesian economics. It may very well be that the book should have put more emphasis on banks, but I am not in a good position to second-guess the editorial decisions behind a best-selling book. Based on online comments by J.W. Mason, his complaint might be closer related to the debate about the importance of net financial assets (Section 5.9). Why this concern was written in the above fashion is not clear, but the wording above is quite similar to other critics in discussing the role of the banking system.

The first thing to immediately note is that MMT proponents hardly ignore banking in other contexts. Chapter 10 of *Macroeconomics* (by Mitchell, Wray, and Watts) has the title "Money and Banking." Eric Tymoigne has a long sequence of primers on banking available at the *New Economic Perspectives* website: (URL: https://neweconomicperspectives.org/money-banking) Note that there is a PDF edition of a long-form version of the tutorial. As such, we see that MMT does not completely ignore banks.

Semantic Gap

The simplest possible explanation for this debate is that Mason and MMT proponents are using "money" to refer to two different things. In particular, MMT proponents can be seen as referring to what is technically known as the monetary base (which consists of currency in circulation and settlement balances at the central bank), while Mason is referring to a broad monetary aggregate (e.g., M1 or M2).

I view the source of this difference as being the perspective taken on analysis of the economy. The MMT perspective is viewing the economy from the point of view of the government, while the opposing view is taking the perspective of a member of the public.

From the perspective of the government, the government has a monopoly over the means of payment – currency in circulation, net positions in the wholesale payments system. Private "moneys" are subordinate, and layered on top of the monetary base. (This is exactly how private money is described in MMT primers, so this is not something that was forgotten.)

Critics seem to be looking at this from the perspective of private sector actors, and thinking about how the private sector settles payments. From this perspective, bank deposits are the primary form of money, with banknotes being used for small transactions. In this case, the government does not appear to have a monopoly.

My concern with this private sector perspective is that it offers no useful information about the economy. Why don't banks float multiple domestic currencies? Why do these private currencies have value, other than the circular argument that they are used in exchange? Why does a floating currency sovereign have no reason to fear default? We are back at the conventional view – which has very clear analytical defects.

In any event, the reader will have to accept that this is a semantic story. One can be distressed that MMT proponent define "money" in a way that does not match one's intuitions. However, complaining about a cosmetic wording issue when people like me have no problems understanding the meaning from context is not particularly impressive. Having written the book *Abolish Money (From Economics)!*, I am not particularly impressed with semantic squabbling about the word "money."

Bank and Government Money Difference Blurry

If we move beyond the semantic argument, the question is whether there is something substantive behind this debate. My feeling is that there is not.

Modern Monetary Theory researchers spent a good deal of time researching the details of monetary operations, both legal and institutional. The summary formula I use is that banks are utilities – their money creation powers are overseen by the state to achieve objectives. The state set up the legal apparatus to give banks a special status, so that this private sector money creation can be concentrated under the eyes of regulators.

In any event, the division between "bank money" and "government money" is largely artificial. Although the private sector can set up rinky-dink payment systems like crypto-currencies, modern industrial capitalism is the story of large entities that send large payments to each other. Taking Canada as an example, that payment system at the time of writing is the Large Value Transfer System (LVTS). (The LVTS is to be replaced by a real-time system.) This payment system is backstopped by the central bank. As stated in a Bank of Canada background document:

> *The Bank of Canada guarantees settlement of payments in the system in the extremely unlikely event that more than one participant fails during the LVTS*

operating day, and the amount owed by the failing participants exceeds the value of collateral pledged to the Bank of Canada.

Banks make payments to and from the LVTS, and have a corresponding balance. Under normal conditions, banks kept their balances as close to zero as possible by the end of the day. (In 2020, the Bank of Canada hopped onto the Quantitative Easing bandwagon and forced its balance to be negative at the end of day, which by implication left the private sector in aggregate with a positive balance. These settlement balances would be called "excess reserves" in American Economics 101 textbook jargon, but that is a misnomer, since Canadian banks do not have a deposit reserve requirement.)

Given the central nature of the wholesale payments system, other forms of money are of secondary importance. (Very few legitimate businesses undertake large transactions with banknotes.) Balances with the payments system are the unit of measurement (account), and there is no difference between "government money" and "bank money": a balance is a balance.

Differences in Money Creation Capability

Despite feverish arguments you see on the internet, bank money creation is hardly a cost-free exercise. Bank money is generally created by extending loans, which is an activity that banks do under the watch of government regulators, which exposes the banks to credit risk. Meanwhile those deposits can depart via the payment system, and the bank needs to have the capacity to raise a countervailing cash flow the same day (except in the case where it is sitting on a large positive settlement balance, which is more common in the era of QE). Banks face very real constraints on money creation, and the government controls many of those constraints.

This is different than the (consolidated) government that is a currency sovereign. It writes a cheque, and the only thing stopping the transfer are self-imposed constraints on intra-governmental accounting. External actors have little say in the matter.

This explains why governments keep bailing out the banking sector, and not the other way around. Given that most MMT primers (like *The Deficit Myth*) are discussing government policy and its constraints, it makes no sense for them to treat bank money as equivalent to government money.

Writing a Cheque to Pay Taxes Doesn't Matter

One argument that I ran into years ago made an argument to the effect that taxes are paid via cheque (or bank transfer), and not with "government money." Furthermore, the means to make payment could have been borrowed from a bank – hence the money was created by the private sector.

As I noted in the discussion of the Monetary Monopoly model in Section 4.3, the use of banks as a payment intermediary does not affect the final result. The bank still needs to acquire government money for the payment to clear. The fact that the private sector layers private claims on top of government money is discussed in the MMT literature, and is obvious to anyone who has ever looked at monetary aggregate data.

Business Cycle Concerns

If the discussion is about the business cycle more generally, then yes, private sector credit growth matters. But it is archaic to argue that bank money creation is of primary importance; we live in a world where credit growth is increasingly in the hands of non-bank financing (also known as shadow banking). That said, this is a change of subject relative to most MMT primers. Given that the usual objective of fiscal policy is to be counter-cyclical, there needs to be other forces that generate the business cycle.

If the complaint is that there is no MMT magic solution to predicting the business cycle, I would respond that every other school of economic thought is in the same boat.

References and Further Reading
- "Can We Create All the Money We Need?" by J.W. Mason, *The American Prospect,* July 14, 2020. URL: https://prospect.org/culture/books/mmt-can-we-create-all-the-money-we-need/
- *Macroeconomics,* by William Mitchell, L. Randall Wray, and Martin Watts. Red Globe Press, 2019. ISBN: 978-1-137-61066-9.
- Posts on Money and Banking, by Eric Tymoigne. (Being developed into a textbook *The Financial System and the Economy: Principles of Money and Banking.* Only a draft version available at the time of writing.) URL: https://neweconomicperspectives.org/money-banking
- Bank of Canada Backgrounders: Large Value Transfer System. URL: https://www.bankofcanada.ca/wp-content/uploads/2010/11/large_value_transfer_system.pdf
- *Abolish Money (From Economics)!* Brian Romanchuk, *BondEconomics.*

ISBN: 978-0-9947480-8-9
- "The Deficit Myth: Banking Between the Lines," by Raul Carrillo, September 9, 2020. URL: https://lpeproject.org/blog/the-deficit-myth-banking-between-the-lines/ (This article came out after I wrote the manuscript section, but it is a response to the J.W. Mason article, with a good overview of the MMT thinking about banking.)

5.8 Post-Keynesian Squabbling

Although MMT can be considered as part of the broad-tent post-Keynesian tradition, this does not imply that other post-Keynesians and MMT proponents necessarily agree with one another. In fact, in terms of substantive criticism, most of it has come from other post-Keynesians. This can be explained that they represent the bulk of critics that have read the MMT scholarly literature.

Since I would prefer to sell books to post-Keynesians as well as MMT supporters, I have no desire to get involved in pointless academic mudslinging There are certainly topics where there are important substantive differences between MMT proponents and their post-Keynesian critics, and those appear in other sections of this book.

RWER Special Issue

The *Real-World Economics Review* published the special issue "Modern Monetary Theory and Its Critics" (Issue #89) on October 1, 2019. (URL: https://rwer.wordpress.com/2019/10/08/rwer-issue-89-modern-monetary-theory-and-its-critics/). This publication is jam-packed with 203 pages of post-Keynesians and MMT proponents discussing MMT. Most quotes within this section come from articles within this issue, although I will end off with comments on another article.

From my perspective, the following quote from Marc Lavoie's essay tells me all I needed to know.

> Let us start with the first issue. MMT, to me, is just part of post-Keynesian economics. I would classify MMT advocates as Institutionalist post-Keynesians, because they are very much concerned with monetary and financial institutions, and in particular the institutional links between the government and the central bank.

We then need to know how post-Keynesian economics functions. As an academic, Marc Lavoie has to be polite – but I am under no such obligation. Very simply, many (not all) post-Keynesians spend a considerable part of their free time disagreeing with each other. For people with a literary view of economics and who like arguing, this is wonderful. For the rest of us, this pattern of behaviour is best viewed as self-destructive.

Marc Lavoie's writings offer *a constructive* view of post-Keynesian economics. It is possible to debate aspects of MMT in good faith. However, I am skeptical about the good faith of some of the contributors to the volume, so I will not attempt a comprehensive overview.

Academic Turf Wars

One major point of contention is the issue of academic priority and contributions. This might be of interest if you are in academia. However, speaking as an ex-academic, I do not see much merit to such debates. At best, such discussions should be left to future generations of academics.

Academic MMT proponents put their contributions as being part of the post-Keynesian school of thought that pre-dates them. The key is that the MMT project is an attempt to create an internally consistent body of thought – which has eluded the factions within broad-tent post-Keynesianism.

From an non-academic perspective, the key observation is that MMT is an internally consistent body of theory that is distinct from the neoclassical project. Who said what and in what order is not really our concern, so long as we recognise that MMT is part of a larger theoretical project.

Semantic Wrangling

As an example of largely semantic wrangling, I would point to the essay by Jan Kregel with the grandiose title "MMT: The Wrong Answer to the Wrong Question." Kregel writes:

> *In this context the response that MMT is the appropriate answer to the currently fashionable question of how to pay for government expenditures to combat environmental risks or more expansive availability of health care is the wrong answer to the wrong question. The real question is still the availability of appropriate resources, and if there are none, the policy process of shifting resources to these uses. As many have noted, in times of war the "technical" problem of finance is easily solved, the real difficulties are in the mobilization and shifting of resources.*

He then argues:

> *In point of fact, the General Theory was not even needed to resolve the "technical" problem of finance; it had already been dealt with in the works of Schumpeter, Bendixen, L. Albert Hahn, Hawtrey as well as von Mises and Hayek, all of whom recognized that the banking system was capable of providing an unlimited amount of finance for expenditure, public or private, by creating liabilities that serve as means of payment.*

I am unconvinced that Kregel's answer is as definitive as he suggests. Attempting to keep all government liabilities solely on the banking system balance sheet would risk destabilising those banks, particularly for countries with non-concentrated banking systems. The political economy issues associated with the coordination of private bank balance sheets with governments could easily more difficult than those associated with interacting with the government bond market.

Next, we need to step back and look at this complaint in light of what I have outlined about MMT. The "financing" question is part of Functional Finance — which MMTers themselves explicitly cite as earlier work. The Kregel article just goes through the history of Keynesian thought without even once discussing what MMTers view as their contributions to the field.

The references tell us how useful a critique of MMT it is: there are 27 references, four of which are to Kregel's own work, and one to living academics who are part of the MMT community.

Insisting that the solutions to economic problems are found in the writings of Keynes, Schumpeter, etc. runs into the real-world problem that those authors' works have been around for a long time, and very few people are convinced that economic problems are in any sense solved.

Consolidation

Another topic comes up periodically — the issue of consolidating the central bank and the fiscal arm (Treasury) of the government. Marc Lavoie was one of the people on the other side of the debate, and he touches on it in his essay.

Consolidation is not some crazy accounting practice, (almost) every single published account by publicly traded corporations are consolidated balance sheets. All consolidation does is put connected entities within a single analytical unit and removes internal accounting entries that have no effect on outside entities.

If we are discussing the analysis of governmental operations, adding intra-governmental accounts just makes the analysis more complicated, and adds zero information about the interaction between the government and the private sector. (In my *sfc_models* Python project, one can substitute a consolidated government sector model with a central bank and a Treasury model – there is no effect on the solution of modelled private sector variables.)

The exception appears to be the possibility of a governmental default. If the central bank has the power to force the Treasury to default, then we need to be more careful with intra-governmental accounting. The problem is that is a big assumption: in the real world, central banks are enmeshed in a complex set of laws and regulations, and they are far less "independent" than breathless neoliberal economists assume. One needs to dig into the operational details to see whether default is possible – and it was the MMT economists who did that digging.

Palley (2020) Article
Thomas Palley is one of the more persistent MMT critics. His article "What's wrong with Modern Money Theory: macro and political economic restraints on deficit-financed fiscal policy" was published just as I was finishing up this manuscript. Although I am not greatly impressed with the quality of the criticism, it covers many of the topics discussed in this chapter. If one wanted a summary critique (without relying on my wording) of major points of dispute, this might be the briefest version.

Palley covers the "there's nothing new" critique (Section 5.12):

> [reference to a figure in the article]... the critique of MMT is that it 'is a mix of old and new, the old is correct and well understood, while the new is substantially wrong' (Palley 2015b, p. 45). MMT's main macroeconomic claim to fame rests on its declaration regarding government's ability to finance spending without recourse to taxation owing to its ability to issue money. In fact, government's ability to create money to finance spending has long been widely recognized by all economists, who have also long recognized that ability gives government considerable extra financial and policy space.

My argument is that saying this is "the main claim to fame" is not even close to true.

The following statement seems to summarise most of issues of concern within the article.

> In the real world, economic policy and policy outcomes are subject to multiple economic concerns and constraints. Those include concerns about govern-

ment bond rates, private credit market long-term interest rates, financial market stability, the balance of payments and the exchange rate, the inflation constraint imposed via the Phillips curve, and policy implementation and policy credibility constraints.

As will be seen, most of these topics overlap the other sections of this chapter. I will finish with some point form notes about this article.

- He objects to MMT's operations analysis as static and does not take into account behavioural relationships. Given that other schools of thought had almost no useful analysis of operations, it is still about the best work in the area available.
- He has concerns about the political biases about MMT, which are not my concern (Section 1.3).
- Palley has an exaggerated fear of money-financed spending, which makes the article generally sound like something written by an internet Austrian in 2010.
- Palley's analysis of interest rates is weak. He observes that even if the central bank pins government bond yields, private sector interest rates can still rise. Basic financial theory tells us that if the risk-free curve is pinned at 0%, private sector rates represent a credit spread. The fair value for a credit spread is the expected default loss (plus liquidity and term premia), and credit spreads tend to tighten during an expansion.
- His discussion of the Job Guarantee shows no signs that he has adapted his Old Keynesian models to the characteristics of the programme.

In summary, I think Palley's article provides a good survey of (reasonable) MMT critiques, but the details of Palley's arguments are weak. There are stronger versions of the arguments to be found, but scattered across multiple articles.

Concluding Remarks

Some of the debates within the set of essays are discussed elsewhere in this book. From the perspective of someone outside the heterodox economic bubble, where the line between MMT and other post-Keynesians is far less interesting than the divide between post-Keynesians and conventional economics.

References and Further Reading
- *Real-World Economics Review*, Issue #89, October 1, 2019. URL: https://rwer.wordpress.com/2019/10/08/rwer-issue-89-modern-monetary-theory-and-its-critics/
- *Post-Keynesian Economics: New Foundations* by Marc Lavoie. Edward Elgar Publishing, Inc., 2014. ISBN: 978-1-78347-582-7. This hefty textbook covers the breadth of post-Keynesian economics at the senior undergraduate/post-graduate level. It is my go-to book for references for many topics within broad MMT or post-Keynesian theory.
- Palley, T. (2020). What's wrong with Modern Money Theory: macro and political economic restraints on deficit-financed fiscal policy, *Review of Keynesian Economics*, 8(4), 472-493. doi: https://doi.org/10.4337/roke.2020.04.02

5.9 Net Financial Asset Skepticism

One area of skepticism about claims by MMT proponents revolves around statements regarding net financial assets. The first thing to note is that part of the discussions revolve around accounting identities, which are true by definition. Arguing about things that are true by definition is somewhat silly.

The legitimate area of discussion is the behavioural implications of the accounting identity. Critics argue that MMT proponents are drawing too strong behavioural implications from it. Since this is a discussion of different people's interpretations of textual statements, there is plenty of room for pointless arguments. I am skeptical about drawing strong implications from accounting identities, but that said, the arguments used by MMT academics in this area made sense to me in context.

The "Accounting Identity"

The accounting identity I am referring to is the argument that central government liabilities represent the *net* financial assets of every other sector. I will refer to this as the "non-government" sector, although it technically includes sub-sovereigns as well as foreign official actors (e.g., foreign central banks) within the external sector.

Why is this so? For every other financial asset in an economy, it is a corresponding liability of another entity in the non-government sector. As such, they all net out to zero.

The implication drawn is typically worded in this fashion: central government debt is issued to meet the savings desires of the private sector (including the external sector).

Equities

One immediate rejoinder is that equities are not normally thought of as a liability. However, for some national accounting treatments, equities are treated as liabilities, and that is how they are being treated here. There are good arguments on both sides of the "is equity really a liability?" argument, but for my purposes, I do not care – this is the definition that was used, and people are free to define terms as they wish (as long as they are clear in setting out the definitions).

As such, the counterpart of liability issuance of the central government is the corresponding change in net financial assets of the non-government sector.

Behavioural Implications?

Can we draw strong behavioural implications from this relationship? I am skeptical about simplistic economic laws of nature, and that is how many critics interpret the statements about net financial assets. My interpretation of the MMT arguments I have seen is that they are operationally similar to points made by Hyman Minsky.

Minsky's argument was straightforward: government liabilities are the only true safe assets in a credit crunch. Since everything else is purchased with credit – even precious metals – all risk asset prices go down at the same time in a credit crunch. The exception is government bond prices, which rise.

The rising prices of government liabilities are a major factor in stabilising the market value of portfolios and allow entities with strong hands to go on a shopping spree – which ultimately puts the floor under risk asset prices. In my view, this is a useful description of the dynamics seen in a financial crisis, as demonstrated in 2008.

I interpret the statements about saving desires as being consistent with this description. Beyond that, I would just suggest caution with regard to the behavioural implications of accounting identities. I am also unable to get enthusiastic about arguments over the technical definition of "savings," which greatly concerns some people.

References and Further Reading
- See the discussion under "Balance Sheet Implications" in Chapter 2 of *Stabilizing an Unstable Economy*, by Hyman P. Minsky. McGraw Hill, 2008 (first edition published in 1986). ISBN: 978-0-07-159299-4.

5.10 Only Applicable to United States?

One common line of criticism relates to what is termed open economy considerations – can the foreign sector create constraints on fiscal policy that are not apparent in closed economy models? One simplistic variation of this is the argument that "MMT only applies to the United States," that is, only a global hegemon that issues the reserve currency can afford to ignore the external sector.

This area of criticism is the most substantive area where other post-Keynesians split with MMT proponents. I would guess that this is where one would draw a dividing line between the two camps (if we put aside pure academic turf war disputes).

The particular argument that it is only applicable to a "reserve currency" is arguably silly when one invokes Japan, at which point epicycles are added to the argument ("the Japanese owe the money to themselves!"). Furthermore, one of the founders of MMT (Bill Mitchell) is Australian and I am Canadian, so if a reserve currency were seen as required, we presumably would have noticed. As such, I will deal with what I see as the good faith version of the critique – that the external sector can impose constraints on fiscal policy. That is, instead of "bond vigilantes" curtailing government spending, "foreign sector vigilantes" will ride into town.

There is a related point – that "MMT is not applicable to developing countries." Finally, I will discuss the "imports are a benefit, exports are a cost" arguments.

Basic Mechanics – Foreigners Have No Privileges

The first thing to note is that foreign bond holders have zero special privileges in the developed countries. Unlike developing countries that issue bonds adjudicated in foreign courts, developed country bonds are mainly issued under local law. (There is a small residual of foreign currency debt, e.g., the Canadian Federal Government issues some U.S. dollar bonds to finance its relatively small foreign exchange reserve.)

Whether a U.S. Treasury is owned by a local or a foreigner makes no operational difference to how payments are made by the Treasury. As such, the residence of owners makes no difference for default risks.

All that can happen is that foreigners who own the government bond can sell, netting them local currency cash. Next, they can trade that cash away in the foreign exchange market.

Exchange Rate Weakness to Domestic Inflation?

The true potential concern is that the domestic currency will lose value in the foreign exchange markets.

In fixed currency regimes, such devaluations were associated with inflation. At the extreme, hyperinflations result from when domestic prices are effectively set in a hard currency terms, and local prices are those foreign prices multiplied by the exchange rate. As the local currency value plunges towards zero (in foreign currency terms), the multiplier goes to infinity. (Academic research on hyperinflations uses foreign exchange quotations to estimate inflation rates, since there is no way of reliably recording the domestic price level when the monthly inflation rate is over 50%.)

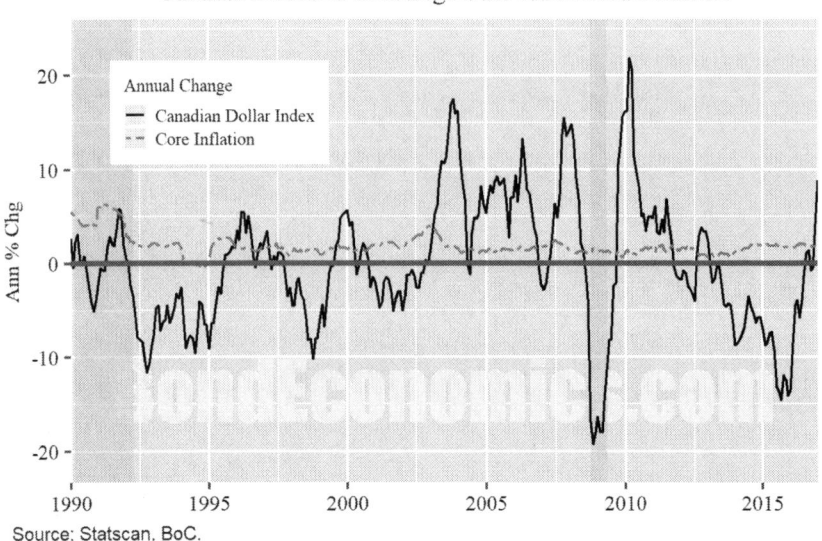

Canada: Effective Exchange Rate Index And Inflation

Source: Statscan, BoC.

However, in an environment where the currency is floating and the economy has achieved inflation stability, currency movements have almost no measurable effect on inflation. The figure above shows the gyrations in the Canadian effective exchange rate index (from the Bank of Canada) for the period 1990-2017. (The available data ends in 2017.) Canada is a small economy that is extremely open to trade, but one with a long experience with floating currency (the Canadian dollar floated long before the demise of Bretton Woods). As is often pointed out by developed economy central bankers, inflation has been stable since the early 1990s – but currency markets continue to oscillate wildly.

There are major differences in opinion among economists as to the importance of the exchange rate on domestic inflation. I would argue that the empirical evidence is that the estimated effects are quite low, whereas the other side typically invokes potential regime shifts that by definition will not be predictable by using historical data.

A Semantic Nothingburger
To what extent this criticism is legitimate, it revolves around the phrasing of how "inflation" constrains fiscal policy: what weight does one put on the external value of the currency? The reality is that MMT proponents do not ignore the external sector (as some critics suggest), rather there is a major disagreement about the relative importance of the currency value in determining the domestic price level.

That said, *the premise of a floating currency is that the price floats.* If policymakers react to every wiggle in the foreign exchange markets, then the government is backing into a *de facto* peg framework. Countries like Canada have moved towards a policy of benign neglect of the exchange rate, and there have been no reasons so far to question that decision.

Managed Trade
Another angle of attack is the question of the management of trade relationships. At a simplified level, one could view post-Keynesians as wanting a do-over on the Bretton Woods negotiations. A new framework of managed trade would be entered into, but this time, there would be more symmetric obligations between surplus and deficit countries.

The desirability of such a system is a political economy question. From the Canadian perspective, such a scheme would effectively be throwing away our national sovereignty. Meanwhile, it is hard to see how Europeans, the Americans, the Japanese, and the Chinese Communist Party will submit to some supranational body that will effectively overrule all domestic policy setting. The political unreality of such a scheme makes it completely unsurprising that MMT proponents spend little time discussing it.

Developing Countries?

An alternative phrasing of the previous arguments is that the insights of MMT cannot be applied to developing countries. These countries allegedly lack the capacity to act as if they have currency sovereignty.

This is a subject on which I have no strong opinions. My experience is with interest rate dynamics in developed countries. Meanwhile, my experience is that whenever someone announces that they are an expert on emerging markets and then offers an opinion on developed country rates markets, they are almost always miserably incorrect. My charitable assumption is that the policy environment for developed economies and developing economies is quite different, and so knowledge may not be transferable.

Stephanie Kelton discusses this topic in Chapter 5 of *The Deficit Myth*, and my thinking matches hers. The rest of this section will outline how I interpret what she wrote. If one wants more information, one would need to dig into the MMT academic literature, which features policy proposals for particular countries. I am certainly not the person to debate the merits of a job programme in India (or similar).

The international trade system did not arrive by accident or solely the result of market forces; it followed arrangements set up after World War II. Although the economists who set them up may have expected different outcomes, the reality is that these arrangements have not been optimal for the masses of the population. Developing countries were pushed into exporting raw materials, while importing critical manufactured goods (like medicines). It should be noted that the countries that did in fact develop – such as on the Asian periphery – did not follow the "free market" solutions peddled by international organisations. Japan (whose economy was flattened in World War II) also pursued an export-driven strategy, but manufacturing was under the close watch of bureaucrats, while financing was the *keiretsu* (convoy) system, with industrial groups financed by a bank.

For the poorer countries, they are trapped by the need to import manufactured goods, which are paid for with "hard" (floating!) currencies. This configuration is a real economic constraint on policy, and no amount of monetary or fiscal wizardry can fix this. I do not see any certain way for poorer countries to converge with the richer countries. They face real constraints, and the MMT literature emphasises the importance of real constraints.

"Imports Are a Benefit, Exports Are a Cost"
One observation that is often made by MMT proponents is that imports are a benefit, while exports are a cost. That is, when a country exports goods and services, it is shipping stuff to foreigners, while imports allows the consumption of output that other countries have spent capital and labour producing.

This typically comes up in the context of the United States, and the periodic scare stories regarding the U.S. trade deficit – which implies a corresponding capital inflow into the United States. The argument implies that the U.S. is getting cheap goods, at the cost of some spreadsheet entries (electronic record of bond holdings). This framing is quite different than the usual one, in which foreigners are getting control of the United States government via lending money to it. (To a certain extent, this debate pops up the most in the United States, as other countries have other preoccupations on the foreign trade front.)

The statements about benefits/costs can be viewed as being equivalent to accounting identities, so it makes little sense to dispute them. Rather, the issue is political implications – should a country aim for a trade surplus? The attitude expressed in the observation sounds too "free trade" leaning for some critics, and thus we are back at the post-Keynesian push for managed trade.

In my experience, some people conflate "floating currencies" with "free trade." The definite MMT preference for a free-floating currency is interpreted as favouring "free trade" versus "protectionism." However, allowing the value of a currency to float does not imply that there are no other restrictions in transactions across borders. After all, the Canadian dollar floated through most of the post-war era, even when Canadian state intervention was at its peak. MMT proponents might lean towards free trade, but that is hardly unusual, particularly in the North American context.

References and Further Reading
- *The Deficit Myth: Modern Monetary Theory and the Birth of the People's Economy*, by Stephanie Kelton. Public Affairs, Hachette Book Group, 2020. ISBN: 978-1-5417-3618-4

5.11 Replication With a Neoclassical Framework?

One of the standard criticisms raised by many neoclassical economists is that there is nothing new to MMT. Given that neoclassical economists and MMT proponents have been arguing loudly online for over a decade, it seems hard to support the view that MMT is a subset of neoclassical economics. (Another weak point in the argument is that the person making it rarely has read any MMT academic work, so the critic is not exactly sure what features are a part of neoclassical economics.)

A slightly less adversarial stance taken is that MMT insights can be replicated by adapting neoclassical methods. I think the answer to that question is: yes and no. Although it seems possible to get parallel results to parts of "narrow MMT," but the integration with broad MMT does not appear to be possible. This is a more plausible story, and the subject of discussion here.

Policy Conclusions: Yes, They Can Overlap

In online discussions of policies, it is quite often possible that a neoclassical economist and an MMT proponent will have the same policy views. In particular, at least among the center-left, there is an acceptance that loose fiscal policy was the best response to the collapse in activity in 2020. Furthermore, the previous neoclassical consensus that monetary policy alone was sufficient for economic stabilisation has weakened.

Having policy views overlap is not particularly surprising. Not many economists now disagree with the view that loosening fiscal policy will increase nominal GDP. As such, one can arrive at the same fiscal policy stance from any number of theoretical directions. If one is concerned with political coalition building, one probably should emphasise the areas of common ground.

However, even if economists agree about a basic principle about policy, there is no guarantee that they will agree about implementation details. In the 2020 pandemic crisis, the lockdown conditions greatly limited policy options, and there were tight time constraints. Under those conditions, each country had very few reasonable options to choose from, and the choices were determined by pre-existing institutions. As such, the scope of disagreement between economists that occupied similar points on the political spectrum was limited. As policy freedom returns, the room for disagreements will grow.

In any event, if one is interested in theory, one needs to be a stickler for theoretical details, and mushing together logically incoherent systems is a bad idea.

Narrow MMT

Many neoclassical economists focus on the policy recommendation of eliminating government bond issuance (Section 3.5). This policy can be captured in a neoclassical model, and from that extremely narrow perspective, they believe that they have captured the essence of MMT. The problem is that this is only one policy recommendation and does not even cover all narrow MMT (never mind broad MMT).

Instead, the closest a single model could do is to replicate the Monetary Monopoly model in a neoclassical framework. (This may have already been done.) Given the simplicity of the model, one could start from the description in Mosler's *White Paper* (Section 4.2) and build it.

There are issues when adapting neoclassical micro-foundations to the Monetary Monopoly Model. In the model, a key price is set by government fiat, and thus cannot be thought of as the result of an equilibrium process.

If the government is pegging the price of a good, things are trivial if we assume that is an aggregate good and the "law of one price" holds. The government sets the price level in every period and the price level can follow any arbitrary trajectory chosen by the government. This would result in an extremely silly model, and MMT proponents like me would mock its reductionist nature. To be semi-plausible, more than one good would need to be introduced.

However, pegging the price of a good is not the usual MMT policy prescription, rather it is the Job Guarantee (where the JG wage is pegged).

In this case, the usual micro-foundations of the household sector would need to be adapted. The usual framework is that households decide upon the number of hours worked, trading off leisure time versus the consumption possibilities offered by increased total wages by working longer hours. *(The implication is that recessions are just workers voluntarily taking vacations, which people like me mock whenever possible, such as I am doing right now.)* The Job Guarantee is not supposed to be a vacation; it is work. As such, it is meant to be fungible with working in the private sector. The problem is that unless the private sector wage is assumed to be equal to the JG wage, the optimal solution is to not work in the Job Guarantee. (If the private sector wage is assumed to be equal to the JG wage – the law of One Price – then the macro model ends up being almost as trivial as the one in which the government sets the price of the composite good.) This does not align with what seems to be the reasonable expectation: if the JG wage is set at a living wage, unemployed people will show up to work in it.

The end result if that a kludge has to be introduced to the microfoundations: there would have to be a purely arbitrary function that splits the hours worked between the Job Guarantee and the private sector, which would presumably be a function of capacity utilisation and the wage differential. This type of kludge is the sort of thing that neoclassical economists insisted was unacceptable in economic theory publications when they seized the means of academic production.

Once this kludge is introduced, it seems entirely possible that the resulting model would end up looking similar to an aggregated model produced by a post-Keynesian (with theoretical differences that only post-Keynesians care about). It seems safe to say that if a Job Guarantee was a serious political possibility in one or more developed countries, such a model might appear.

Assuming such a model was developed, it is a safe bet that it would be the focus of interest for mainstream economists. Since it does not yet exist, I obviously cannot say how accurately it represents MMT thinking. As the next section will elaborate, it will certainly not represent *all* of MMT. However, for something like the analysis of a Job Guarantee, having more bodies around the table doing empirical work has to be a welcome development.

For many people, having mathematical models to discuss makes them happier. From an academic standpoint, mathematical models do provide an easier way to distinguish work – is the model different? It is much harder to judge originality of a textual argument. However, for those of us who are not in academia, this advantage is not important, and the limited success of mathematical economic models in practice means that we should not focus on them to the detriment of our understanding of the economy.

Broad MMT: Not Really

Realistically speaking, forcing a Job Guarantee into a neoclassical model is as far as the convergence would go. Beyond that, we are drifting into Broad MMT. As discussed in Section 4.6, the only thing that post-Keynesians can reliably agree on is that practically every aspect of the neoclassical theoretical tradition is incorrect.

Neoclassicals do relax some of their questionable theoretical assumptions, but the framework only accepts a small number of changed assumptions at a time (as tractability of the model will break). Throwing every assumption into the trash bin simultaneously is a step too far. Furthermore if every single contested assumption is eliminated, it is very hard to define the resulting model as "neoclassical" – it would just be a post-Keynesian model that has been re-written.

That said, one could imagine that a theoretical revolution on the order of the transition from Old Keynesian thinking to New Keynesian thinking could happen, and the neoclassical foundations are warped in a fashion to incorporate post-Keynesian criticism.

Convergence?

Based on the tendency of neoclassical authors to produce floods of papers on any topic, it seems entirely possible that the neoclassical framework will be adapted to generate results that appear similar to MMT – at least from the perspective of the people who built the models. If we are lucky, such developments could allow for more sensible debates.

However, in the absence of such work, there are enough theoretical divergences that imply that existing neoclassical theory does not cover all insights from MMT.

5.12 Nothing New?

To close off the book, we will now cover a phrase that often appears in complaints about MMT: there is nothing new. Given the large amounts of arguing described previously, this charge is curious. However, there are two angles that are plausible subjects for debate: narrow academic concerns, and policy suggestions.

Academic Turf Wars

One can find post-Keynesian and neoclassical academics exclaiming that there is nothing new to MMT. (One popular version is that everything is either non-original or incorrect.)

I used to be a rather stuffy academic, and not a huge fan of overreach in claims about academic work. From what I have seen of the MMT academic literature, it meets the usual standard for original work that is applied within the field. From an outside perspective, the post-Keynesian/

MMT arguments look like yet another theoretical splitting within the fractious post-Keynesian community, and so arguments about originality need to be taken with a grain of salt. Neoclassical critics also often say the same thing, but these critics typically do not offer evidence that they read the relevant academic work.

My view is that academia – across all fields – is stuck in a dysfunctional state because of unrealistic quantitative targets for publications. If every school of thought is producing too many academic papers, it is easy to find targets for criticism.

From the perspective of the question at hand, all that really matters is that MMT is a blending together of various lines of thought within post-Keynesian economics, with a key identifying characteristic of the importance of central governments being the monopoly supplier of the domestic currency. The importance of the tradition is noted right in the beginning of the description of MMT within the text by Mitchell, Wray, and Watts (page 13)

> *As we will see, MMT builds on the insights of many economists who have worked in the heterodox tradition.*

Policy Novelty

My interpretation of the "there's nothing new" complaints by those outside of academia is that the complaint references policy recommendations. The issue is that if we stop at high level generalisations, it is unsurprising that differing schools of thought will blur together. To make a fair comparison, we need to dig a little.

The first axis to consider is political. As discussed in Section 1.3, MMT activists lean progressive. As such, conservatives will just view MMT as another progressive faction.

The more interesting axis is novelty in policy implementation.

First consider fiscal policy. At the broadest level, one could note that MMT proponents – like other post-Keynesians – prefer fiscal policy to monetary policy for management of the business cycle. A fiscal conservative critic would likely stop at this point and argue that MMT is just a repeat of the Old Keynesian policies. Of course, this requires ignoring everything that MMT proponents are saying about fiscal policy.

If we dig a bit further, one might argue that MMT is just Functional Finance, which is an old theory (and MMT sources note that history). Of course, this ignores the rest of Broad MMT, but one might argue that the Functional Finance aspect of MMT is the most interesting for many people.

The MMT academics note that there are operational and theoretical differences between Functional Finance and MMT, rather MMT uses some of the basic concepts of Functional Finance, but the details differ. Randall Wray wrote a working paper discussing the evolution of Functional Finance in the thinking of Hyman Minsky and Abba Lerner and argues that MMT thinking is closer to the evolution of Minsky's thought.

Finally, there are popular fears about "money printing" and the alleged hyperinflationary risks thereof. The idea is that MMT is not new, as hyperinflationary policies happened historically. As discussed in Section 5.3, these fears are based upon misrepresentation of the MMT position. Critics worried about "money printing" have a hard time discussing this topic, since they never cite the MMT literature. The only policy that almost fits the bill is the abolition of the bond market, permanently locking interest paid at zero. The implications of this policy stance are invariably not examined – rising interest costs cannot fuel a spending spiral. There are potential criticisms of this policy, but it is a novel policy, and has to be examined as such.

Concluding Remarks

Given the number of theoretical debates that have come up in this text, it seems inherently silly to say that there is nothing new to MMT. That stance only makes sense if we keep discussions of economic policies at an extremely generic level (e.g., "MMT encourages the use of fiscal policy"), but that ignores the theoretical aspects highlighted by proponents (the Job Guarantee, fiscal sustainability analysis, etc.).

Otherwise, the statements might refer to academic turf wars. For those of us with the luxury of being bystanders to those conflicts, we have no reason to worry about who said what first. Rather, the question is trying to find ideas that help us make sense of the economy.

References and Further Reading
- "Functional Finance: A Comparison of the Evolution of the Positions of Hyman Minsky and Abba Lerner" by L. Randall Wray. *Levy Institute* Working Paper 900, January 2018. URL: http://www.levyinstitute.org/pubs/wp_900.pdf

End Matter

The following books are ones that I used in my research and reading. Most are by MMT academics, but there are a couple of post-Keynesians texts. There are many introductory primers available for MMT, but the focus here is on more advanced texts.

As for journal articles, some key ones are listed within the body of this book. I would point the reader to the list maintained by the *Gower Initiative of Modern Money Studies* at https://gimms.org.uk/tools-and-resources/ Once one has found a few articles of interest, it should be easy to follow reference chains to get a fuller picture of journal research.

Books that were consulted or referred to include the following.

- *Macroeconomics*, by William Mitchell, L. Randall Wray, and Martin Watts. Red Globe Press, 2019. ISBN: 978-1-137-61066-9
- *Full Employment Abandoned: Shifting Sands and Policy Failures*, William Mitchell and Joan Muysken. Edward Elgar Publishing, 2008. ISBN: 978-1-85898-507-7
- *The Deficit Myth: Modern Monetary Theory and the Birth of the People's Economy*, by Stephanie Kelton. PublicAffairs, Hachette Book Group, 2020. ISBN: 978-1-5417-3618-4
- *The Case for a Job Guarantee*, by Pavlina R. Tcherneva. *Polity Press*, 2020. ISBN: 13-978-1-5095-4211-6.
- *Understanding Modern Money: The Key to Full Employment and Price Stability* by L. Randall Wray. Edward Elgar, 1998. ISBN: 978-1-84542-941-6
- *Seven deadly innocent frauds of economic policy*, by Warren Mosler. Davin Patton, 2010. (I did not discuss this book, rather I focussed on Warren Mosler's *White Paper*.)
- *Soft currency economics*, by Warren Mosler. West Palm Beach, FL: Adams, Viner and Mosler, 1995.
- *Modern Monetary Theory: A Primer on Macroeconomics for Sovereign Monetary Systems* by L. Randall Wray. Palgrave-Macmillan, 2012. ISBN: 978-1-137-26514-2.
- *Eurozone dystopia: groupthink and denial on a grand scale*, by William

Mitchell. Edward Elgar Publishing, 2015. ISBN: 978-1-78471-666-0
- *Modern Monetary Theory and European Macroeconomics*, by Dirk H. Ehnts, *Routledge*, 2017. ISBN: 978-1-315-62303-0
- *Post-Keynesian Economics: New Foundations*, by Marc Lavoie. Edward Elgar Publishing, 2014. ISBN: 978-1-78347-582-7
- *Monetary Economics: An Integrated Approach to Credit, Money, Income, Production and Wealth (Second Edition)*, by Wynne Godley and Marc Lavoie. Palgrave-Macmillan, 2012. ISBN: 978-0-230-30184-9.

Code used to generate figures in this text is available at https://github.com/brianr747/brian_books. The code uses an open source platform found at: https://github.com/brianr747/platform. The platform code imports data from various free databases on the internet.

About the Author

Brian Romanchuk founded BondEconomics.com in 2013. It is a website dedicated to providing analytical tools for the understanding of the bond markets and monetary economics.

He previously was a senior fixed income analyst at *la Caisse de dépôt et placement du Québec*. He held a few positions, including being the head of quantitative analysis for fixed income. He worked there from 2006-2013. Previously, he worked as a quantitative analyst at BCA Research, a Montréal-based economic-financial research consultancy, from 1998-2005. During that period, he developed a number of proprietary models for fixed income analysis, as well as covering the economies of a few developed countries.

Brian received a Ph.D. in Control Systems Engineering from the University of Cambridge, and held post-doctoral positions there and at McGill University. His undergraduate degree was in electrical engineering, from McGill. He is a CFA charter holder.

Brian currently lives in the greater Montréal area.

Also By BondEconomics
Understanding Government Finance

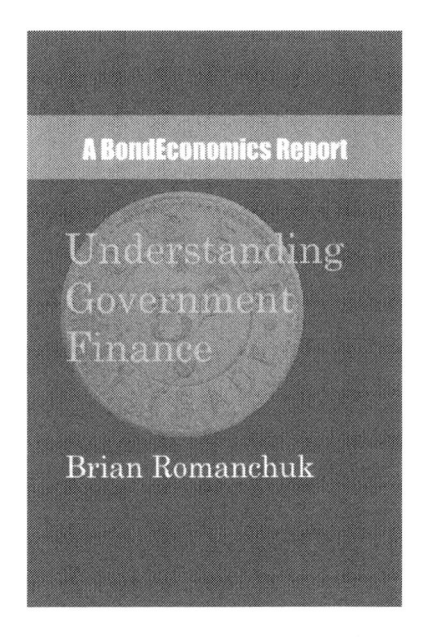

The government budget is not like a household budget. This report introduces the financial operations used by a central government with a free-floating currency, and explains how they differ from that of a household or corporation. The focus is on the types of constraints such a government faces. This report introduces a simplified framework for the monetary system, along with the operating procedures that are associated with it. Some of the complications seen in real-world government finance are then added onto this simplified framework. This report also acts as an introduction to some of the concepts used by Modern Monetary Theory, a school of thought within economics. Modern Monetary Theory emphasises the real limits of government action, as opposed to purely theoretical views about fiscal policy.

Interest Rate Cycles: An Introduction

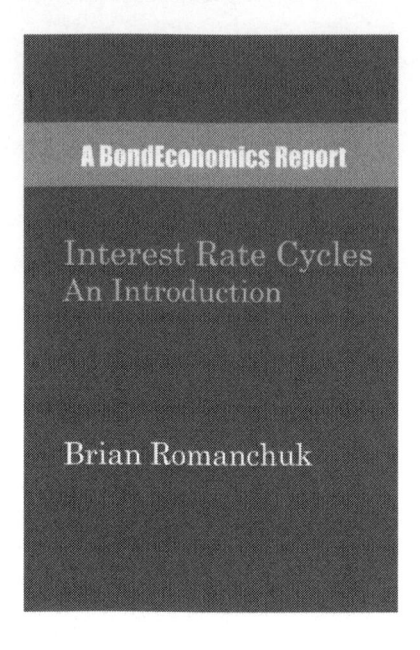

Monetary policy has increasingly become the focus of economists and investors. This report describes the factors driving interest rates across the economic cycle. Written by an experienced fixed income analyst, it explains in straightforward terms the theory that lies behind central bank thinking. Although monetary theory appears complex and highly mathematical, the text explains how decisions still end up being based upon qualitative views about the state of the economy. The text makes heavy use of charts of historical data to illustrate economic concepts and modern monetary history. The report is informal, but contains references and suggestions for further reading.

Abolish Money (From Economics)!

A BondEconomics Report

Abolish Money (From Economics)!

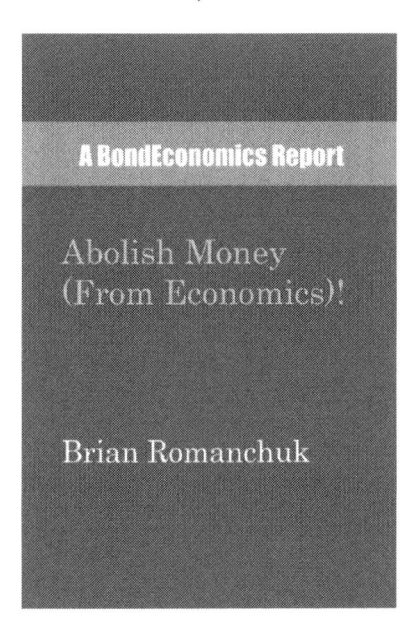

Brian Romanchuk

We live in a monetary economy, so it is not surprising that money plays an important role within economic theory. The argument of this book is that this role has become too important, and has warped our ability to think about the economy. The important psychological role of money within society has been transferred to monetary aggregates, and they are given far more significance than they deserve. Economists have wasted considerable time discussing reforms to the monetary system, such as Quantitative Easing, Positive Money, and Helicopter Money. We need to instead focus our attention on non-monetary reforms. This book consists of 22 essays that discuss the role of money within economic theory, and the controversies raised by debates about the role of money. The tone is informal, as the theoretical debates are translated into plain language.

An Introduction to SFC Models Using Python

Stock-Flow Consistent (SFC) models are a preferred way to present economic models in the post-Keynesian tradition. This book gives an overview of the sfc_models package, which implements SFC models in Python. The approach is novel, in that the user only specifies the high-level parameters of the economic model, and the framework generates and solves the implied equations. The framework is open source, and is aimed at both researchers and those with less experience with economic models. This book explains to researchers how to extend the sfc_models framework to implement advanced models. For those who are new to SFC models, the book explains some of the basic principles behind these models, and it is possible for the reader to run example code (which is packaged with the software online) to examine the model output.

Breakeven Inflation Analysis

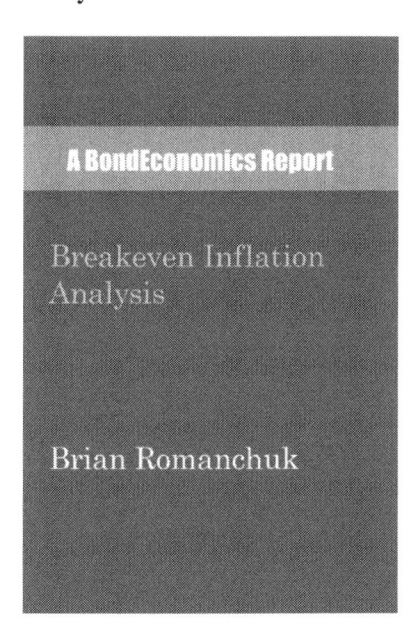

The great inflation of the 1970s in the developed countries provoked strong economic (and political) reactions. In finance, investors searched for ways to protect themselves from inflation. The United Kingdom launched the first modern inflation-linked bonds in 1981. In addition to being of interest to investors looking for protection against inflation, these bonds also provide a market-based measure of inflation expectations. Since investors have "skin in the game," the resulting forecasts might be better than a purely survey-based inflation forecast. More reliable inflation forecasts should be useful for policymakers that aim to control inflation.

This report discusses the breakeven inflation rate that is implied by pricing in the fixed income markets.

Recessions: Volume I

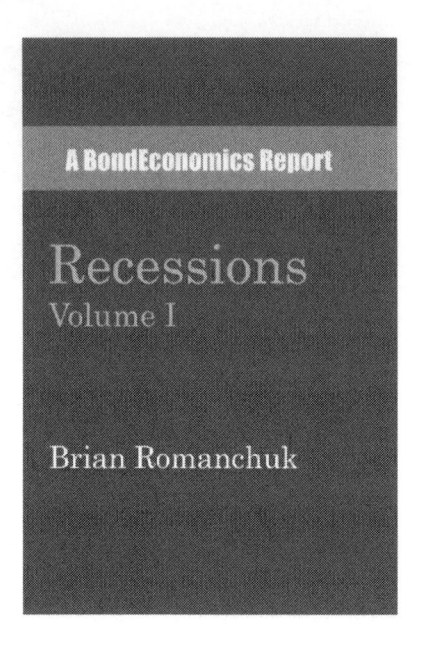

This book looks at the theory of recessions from a (mainly) post-Keynesian perspective. What are the mechanisms behind recessions, and what do various theories or models predict?

This volume is what might be described as a "guided survey": there is a theoretical narrative, but it is developed by surveying existing theories. The writing style is at an intermediate level, being at about the same complexity as what might be seen in the business press, but with a large body of footnotes/endnotes to point readers to academic papers.

The main theoretical argument is that recessions are inherently hard to forecast. Anyone who has read financial market commentary for an extended period will not be surprised by this; missed recession calls are a pervasive phenomenon. The interesting question is: why are recessions hard to forecast? The mechanisms outlined in this book help explain why theory suggests that this should be so.

Index

A

academic turf wars 127, 141–142
administered price 91–94
affordability 108
Albrecht, Brian C. 113
American Debt Ceiling Fiasco of 2013 37
An introduction to SFC Models Using Python 87
automatic stabilisers 118

B

Bank of Canada 123
banks 5, 79, 121–125
barter 97
Bernanke, Ben 15
bond 64
  abolition of 64–65
  as a reserve drain 3
  yield 16, 88

C

Canada 38, 41, 135
central bank 44
Congressional Budget Office (CBO) 28, 87
consolidation 64, 128–129
credit controls 120
currency sovereign 4, 37, 73, 137

D

debt ceiling 66. See also *American Debt Ceiling Fiasco of 2013*
debt-to-GDP ratio 85–86
developing countries 136

E

Edesess, Michael 110–111
euro 64
external sector 133–136

F

falsifiability 34–36
Farmer, Roger E. 36
financing constraint 3
fiscal policy 49–52
  active 117–119
  austerity 37–41
  budget constraint 83
  budgeting 119
  financing procedures 63–66
  time consistency 113–114
fiscal sustainability 82–87
Fiscal Theory of the Price Level 81
fish 111
flex price 91
Full Employment Abandoned (book) 19, 20, 26, 32, 34
full employment framework 19
Fullwiler, Scott 49, 83, 88, 93, 106–107, 119
Functional Finance 2, 49, 51, 95, 143

G

Galí, Jordi 80
governmental budget constraint 83
Gower Initiative of Modern Money Studies 97
Great Moderation 15
Greece 40
Green New Deal 10, 61–63
Grey, Rohan 66, 93, 99, 119

H

hyperinflation 52, 63, 115, 134
hysteresis 34

I

inflation 29–31, 32, 44, 51, 55–56, 90–96, 114, 134
  administrative controls 119–120
  cost push 92
inflation constraint 3, 49, 117
Inflation Targeting 43–45
interest rates 65, 88–89

skepticism 45–46, 74–75

J

Job Guarantee 4, 10, 51, 53–60, 62, 79, 93, 115, 139
   criticisms 57–58

K

Kalecki, Michal 92
Kelton, Stephanie 38, 136
Klein, Matthew C. 108–109
Kregel, Jan 127

L

labour disputes 21–22
Lavoie, Marc 6, 98, 126
Lee, Frederic 99–100
Lerner, Abba P. 2
Levey, Sam 78

M

Macroeconomics (book) 6, 92, 119, 122, 142
Mason, J.W. 121–122
Mejia, Jackson 113
microeconomics 99–100
Minsky, Hyman 39, 60, 132
Mitchell, William 4, 6, 15, 19, 33, 34, 133
MMT. See Modern Monetary Theory
Modern Monetary Theory
   Broad 6–7, 96–101, 140
   legal analysis 99
   Narrow 2–5, 72, 139
Monetary Monopoly Model 51, 76–78, 94
monetary operations 4, 73–74
monetary policy 45–46
money 97, 123
money printing 5, 67, 106–107, 143
Mosler, Warren 4, 55, 72
   White Paper 72–75, 139
Mucha, Carlos 66
Muysken, Joan 19, 33

N

NAIRU 26–31, 28, 32, 35, 94
neoclassical economics 80, 83, 100–101, 138–140
net financial asset 131
New Zealand 44
nothingburger 135

O

OECD Jobs Study 19–20

P

Palley, Thomas 129–130
pandemic 13, 69, 138
politics 8–10, 101, 105
post-Keynesian 51, 90, 126–130
   broad tent 6, 98–99
price level 73, 75–82
PZIRP 75

R

r^* 36
r-g 85–86

S

SFC models. See stock-flow consistent models
Spain 41
stock-flow consistent models 5, 99
structural reform 34

T

Tankus, Nathan 91, 93, 119
tax 3
Tcherneva, Pavlina R. 23, 32, 53, 56, 61, 76
The Case for a Job Guarantee (book) 32, 53–58, 61
The Deficit Myth (book) 38, 122, 136
time consistency. See fiscal policy: time consistency
Tlaib, Rashida 66
trillion-dollar coin 66
Tymoigne, Eric 122

U

Understanding Government Finance (book) 64, 83, 108
unemployment 28
  long-term 23
  natural rate 27
  structural 33
  under-employment 24
United States 28, 30–31, 133, 137
Universal Basic Income 59–60

W

Watts, Martin 6
Widowmaker Trade 9
Wray, L. Randall 6, 76, 97, 143

Printed in Great Britain
by Amazon